Halifax
From Front-Line Bomber to Post-War Transport

Key Books

HISTORIC MILITARY AIRCRAFT SERIES, VOLUME 29

Published by Key Books
An imprint of Key Publishing Ltd
PO Box 100
Stamford
Lincs PE9 1XQ

www.keypublishing.com

Original editions published as *Aeroplane Icons: Halifax*
© 2013, edited by Barry Charles Wheeler

This edition © 2023

ISBN 978 1 80282 477 3

Typeset by SJmagic DESIGN SERVICES, India.

Contents

Introduction

One of the three British four-engine heavy bombers which took the night war to Hitler's heartland, the Handley Page Halifax contributed in no small way to the destruction and ultimate surrender of the Third Reich. Unlike its Short Stirling and Avro Lancaster companions, the Halifax proved a more versatile design, taking on roles additional to its principal mission with RAF Bomber Command. Yet its comparatively short period in service and a production run of 6,176 machines was not without problems.

In its early years from service entry in March 1941, little good could be said about the Halifax. Its in-built faults found it underpowered, its performance was lamentable, it suffered from a vicious swing on take-off causing inherent undercarriage collapses, and rudder stall problems often gave fatal results. All round it was a poor design from Britain's most famous builder of big bombers! In fact, so bad was the aircraft that 'Bomber' Harris wanted it withdrawn from service and production switched in favour of the Lancaster. Indeed, his opinion of owner Frederick Handley Page bordered on the murderous!

Given Britain's emergency war production such a radical move was unthinkable. Across the nation, hundreds of factories large and small were heavily committed to a massive programme supplying Halifax parts to four huge construction plants laid down to produce this heavyweight for the RAF. There was simply no time or money to switch to building a new machine. Instead, Handley Page designers struggled to improve their unfortunate offspring and it was a good two years before they succeeded.

To the public, the Halifax was the highly capable stablemate of the Lancaster and together, the two four-engine machines were hailed as the fearsome harbingers of doom aimed at laying waste all that was evil within the Third Reich. But the day of the Halifax proved worth waiting for.

New engines, a strengthened structure and modified aerodynamics gave the aeroplane the performance that had been promised two years earlier. The Mk III proved faster than the Lancaster and could climb quicker; by late-1944, Halifax losses dropped below those of the Lancaster, even though the former often outnumbered the latter on some of the big raids. Total figures for Bomber Command were 2,236 Halifax losses against 3,936 Lancasters.

Those who flew and maintained the Halifax were largely loyal to the type, particularly the Canadians who operated 15 squadrons. Its early difficulties overcome, the design was found ideal for other tasks – towing gliders, carrying troops, stuffing the fuselage full of electronics to spook the enemy, anti-submarine patrollers, spy dropping and in the post-war world, flying early civil air routes around Europe and helping to sustain Berlin against the Russians.

This book reviews the lows and highs of the mighty Halifax – all 6,178 built including the prototypes – and recounts its contribution to the Allied success in winning the Second World War.

Chapter 1

Blue Bird to Halifax

Frederick Handley Page, remembered in his later years for grand pre-war airliners, heavy wartime bombers and crescent-winged four-jet warplanes, was born in the age of balloons and hand-flown models. His birthplace was Cheltenham, Gloucestershire, where, on November 15, 1885, he became the second of four sons of furniture-maker Frederick Page and his wife Ann Eliza, nee Handley. Young Frederick trained as an electrical engineer but his interest through his teenage years centred increasingly on model aeroplanes and steadily moved towards a desire to build and fly his own aircraft.

Exploring various ideas and having long discussions with some early gliding pioneers, it was the demonstrations in Europe by American Wilbur Wright in 1908 that fired Handley Page to form the world's first public company to build gliders at Barking, on June 17, 1909. Constructing a glider and

A young Frederick Handley Page sitting in his first tractor monoplane, Bluebird, in April 1910; self-taught, he flew it briefly in a straight hop the following month, on May 26. The engine was a 20hp Advance vee-four air-cooled unit which proved highly temperamental. (via Barry Charles Wheeler)

Two-spar crescent wings and a tapering fuselage with tandem seats gave the 1911 Type E monoplane a handsome appearance. Called Yellow Peril, it was flown by Edward Petre on July 24, 1912, and went on to give many people their first experience of flying before being converted into a single-seater in 1914. It survived until 1940 when its decrepit remains were finally scrapped. (via Barry Charles Wheeler)

making propellers and accessories, he built his first powered aircraft, the Type A Blue Bird monoplane which he flew for the first time, with no previous instruction or training, on May 26, 1910. The improved Type D Yellow Peril followed in time for static display at the third Aero Show at Olympia in April 1911. It flew on July 15, but the pilot, Robert Fenwick, crashed it on landing, much to the annoyance of Handley Page.

A move to larger premises at Cricklewood Lane, North London, took place in September 1912 where HP constructed further designs, both monoplanes and biplanes incorporating curved Weiss-type wing shapes. He reserved a flight shed at nearby Hendon and as he expanded his work force, so he hired George Rudolph Volkert, an engineering graduate who was appointed chief designer at the wage of 15 shillings a week. Volkert's first design was the two-seat Type G which flew in November 1913.

With the declaration of war in August 1914, HP was approached by Commodore Murray Sueter of the Admiralty to discuss plans for a long-range bombing and coast patrol aeroplane capable of attacking the German High Seas Fleet in its base at Kiel and the growing number of Zeppelin sheds appearing along the Friesian coast.

In 1915, HP designer George Rudolph Volkert gave the Admiralty its 'bloody paralyser' in the form of the HP 0/100 bomber. The wings spanned 114ft and six 100lb bombs could be carried in the centre fuselage. Each costing less than £5,000, this big 'twin' was the harbinger of many more large designs from the company stretching over more than 40 years. The 0/100 seen here was fitted with two back to back 200hp Hispano-Suiza engines which led to the improved 0/400. (via Barry Charles Wheeler)

Meanwhile, Commander Charles Samson, who had attempted to prevent the German take-over of Antwerp, unsuccessfully as it turned out, signalled back to Sueter 'What we want here is a bloody paralyser to stop the Hun in his tracks', a message Sueter gave to Handley Page who, with Volkert, designed the Type O/100. This was to be powered by two engines, carry up to six 110lb bombs stowed in an internal fuselage bay and have a crew of two. For a company which up until that time had only produced small two-seaters, a 100ft span bomber was a huge step into the unknown.

However, by February 1915, the all-wood structural design was established and the Admiralty ordered four prototypes and eight production aircraft, later increased to a total of 42. HP rapidly took on more workers and by November, the payroll had risen to 150 and the first aircraft, fitted with 250hp Rolls-Royce V12 engines, later named Eagle and shortly developed to 320hp, was towed the three-quarter mile journey (which took five hours due to the dismantling of trees, poles and lights) to Hendon. On December 17, 1915, the first great Handley Page bomber made its initial flight in the hands of Lt Cdr John Babington and Lt Cdr Ernest Stedman, lifting off at 50mph before landing safely within the airfield boundary.

Left: Sir Frederick Handley Page, founder of the world's first public company solely for the construction of aeroplanes on June 17, 1909. Born in Cheltenham, Gloucestershire, on November 15, 1885, and trained as an electrical engineer, he is best remembered for his pioneering development of large aircraft in the early days of aviation for both military and commercial use. He was knighted in 1942 and lived to see his mighty jet-powered Victor bomber in RAF service. He died on April 21, 1962, aged 77. (*Aeroplane*)

Below: Ground crew towing an 0/400 bomber at Ligescourt, France, halt briefly for the War Office photographer to take this picture. A Clayton tractor is doing most of the work hitched to the aircraft of No 207 Sqn RAF – the date was August 29, 1918. (via Barry Charles Wheeler)

Above: To attack the enemy capital, Berlin, from Britain, the V/1500 was designed – larger than the 0/400 and capable of carrying twice the load with four engines. On November 9, 1918, three production examples were ready for the first raid by No 166 Sqn RAF of the Independent Force, but before it could take place, two days later the Armistice was signed and the operation was cancelled. The picture shows one of the completed V/1500s. (via Barry Charles Wheeler)

Right: Having formed Handley Page Transport Ltd to operate converted 0/400s on commercial routes between Britain and the Continent, HP designed and built the W.8 biplane airliner in 1920 to further develop civil flying. The W.8b and W.8C followed with the larger W.8f Hamilton appearing in 1924. Passenger accommodation rose from 12 to 16 and inside, two-abreast seating with curtains and wall-lights added a touch of sophistication for those intrepid early travellers. (via Barry Charles Wheeler)

Pilot and nose gunner of a Royal Air Force 0/400 bomber. Exposed to the elements, the former gained some protection from the slanted windscreens, but even at 97mph the gunner experienced a grimly miserable position to fend off enemy fighters. (via Barry Charles Wheeler)

On May 27, 1916, the Royal Naval Air Service took formal delivery of the second prototype and flew it to the new military airfield at Manston, Kent, for trials. Changes and modifications found the O/100 capable of uplifting up to 16 112lb bombs with a crew increased to four and a Handley Page Training Flight was formed in September 1916.

The first bombing raid by the type took place on March 16/17, 1917, when Babington attacked a railway junction at Metz. Much modified, the O/100 became the famous O/400 when engines of increased power – two 360hp R-R Eagle VIIIs – greater airframe strength, and a revised fuel system resulted in a machine capable of a maximum speed of 95mph and a service ceiling of 8,500ft. The O/400 was the first British bomber to undertake an 81/2hr flight when Flt Cdr F Digby bombed Cologne on March 24/25, 1918. O/400 deliveries totalled 554.

For Handley Page's next aeroplane, the V/1500, the overall size increased to meet a military requirement for an aircraft to fly from England to attack Berlin, Britain's first true strategic bomber. With a wingspan of 126ft, four 375hp Rolls-Royce Eagle VIII engines mounted back to back, and a capacity for 30 250lb bombs, the V/1500 was a giant of its time. Construction of the first aircraft took place in secret at Harland & Wolf in Belfast under the direction of Volkert, the prototype being returned to Cricklewood for erection and a first flight on May 22, 1918, only eight months from inception.

Seven production aircraft had reached the two squadrons (No 166 and 167) which formed 86 Wing of the RAF's new Independent Force with three preparing to conduct the type's first raid on Berlin when the Armistice was signed on November 11, 1918. Thus, the planned operational debut of the type was cancelled. However, four days later, the big V/1500 achieved a historical 'first' when it carried a group of journalists and several employees totalling 40 passengers in the capacious fuselage up to

6,500ft over Cricklewood, the most people any aircraft had flown at that time. The end of the war brought extensive cuts in defence and only 60 of 210 V/1500s were completed, most going straight into store before being broken up.

With the Armistice, Handley Page turned to commercial operations and in June 1919 Handley Page Transport was established to begin scheduled services between London (Hounslow, later Croydon) and Paris with converted O/400s. This led to the purpose-built 16-seat W.8 biplane airliner, the improved W.8e/f Hamilton, the W.9 Hampstead and the larger W.10, based on the military Hyderabad. All flew with Imperial Airways into which HP Transport had merged in 1924.

A chunky, two-seat day bomber, the HP.28 Handcross prototype (J7498) was flown on December 6, 1924, and was the first of three built to meet an RAF requirement. The engine was a Rolls-Royce Condor which gave a top speed of 120mph and a range of 500 miles with a 550lb bomb recessed in a ventral fairing. However, the RAF rejected the Handley Page design, preferring Hawker's more capable Horsley instead. (via Barry Charles Wheeler)

Moves and Majesty

In November 1929, Handley Page vacated the airfield at Cricklewood, but retained the factory, and moved to a new site at Radlett in Hertfordshire, establishing large erection sheds and drawing offices, the new site being officially opened on July 7, 1930. The great triumph for Handley Page among the inter-war airliners was undoubtedly the H.P.42 – the Hannibal/Heracles class – powered by four radial engines, two above and two below the sizeable biplane wings and considered by many travellers of the time to be the most comfortable of all to fly in. Ten were built and although accidents happened, no passengers were killed on Imperial's scheduled services.

Aerodynamic advances saw the successful development of the Handley Page slot which improved air flow over the wing at high angles of attack, to delay the stall. This device was tested on a Bristol Fighter and patented, bringing additional funds into the company.

As the Guggenheim Competition Biplane – shortened by the Press to Gugnunc – the HP.39 demonstrated Handley Page's innovative slotted wing which improved airflow over the aerofoil at slow speed and high angles of attack, thus delaying the stall. It flew in the 1929 Guggenheim Competition and came second to the American Curtiss Tanager, also fitted with the HP slots. Handley Page earned over £650,000 in patent rights for the design. Today, the unique Gugnunc still survives in the British Science Museum collection. (via Barry Charles Wheeler)

Aimed at a specification for a deck-landing torpedo-carrier, the HP.19 Hanley was designed by ST Richards to take advantage of the latest slotted wing, considered ideal for the rigours of carrier-based operations. Various changes were undertaken during trials at the Martlesham Heath experimental establishment, the third Hanley I, N145, seen here in April 1922 showing clearly the full-span slots on the leading edge of the wings. (via Barry Charles Wheeler)

Through the 1920s, Handley Page secured contracts for a number of different aircraft for military use, some of which did not reach production. The Hanley, Hendon and Harrow torpedo carriers, the Handcross and Hare day bombers, and other types which were not blessed with names such as the H.P.43 transport, H.P.46 and the H.P.47, even a fleet fighter monoplane for the US Navy, the H.P.21. But now firmly associated as a builder of big bombers, the company continued its earlier success with supplying the RAF with a series of biplane bombers, namely the Hyderabad, Hinaidi and Heyford, all three entering service between 1925 and 1933.

Back to Bombers

In 1932, design started on the first Handley Page monoplane bomber, the H.P.52 Hampden. This was to the same requirement for which Vickers submitted the Wellington and both companies received production contracts. Given the soubriquet 'Flying Suitcase' by the irascible Editor of the Aeroplane magazine, CG Grey, because of its narrow fuselage 'nacelle' and tapering tail boom, the four-seat Hampden with Bristol Pegasus XVIII radial engines could carry up to 4,000lb of bombs.

Two prototypes of the Harrow torpedo-bomber were built, the first flying on April 24, 1926. The 470hp Napier Lion V engine was later replaced by a 530hp unit for the Harrow II, but even its good handling characteristics failed to win over the Air Ministry and no order was placed. (via Barry Charles Wheeler)

Based on the HP.51, the Harrow was produced to an Air Ministry requirement for a monoplane bomber with a crew of five. The prototype flew on October 10, 1936, and 100 were ordered, the type entering RAF service with No 214 Sqn at Scampton only three months later in January 1937. However, as a front-line bomber, the Harrow's career was brief – by December 1939, Wellingtons had replaced them, and they were switched to transport and training duties. (via Barry Charles Wheeler)

Having a better performance than the Hyderabad, the similar Hinaidi incorporated metal construction, two Bristol Jupiter radial engines in place of the earlier Napier Lions, a crew of four and the capacity to carry 1,568lb of bombs. Both types retained a wing span of 75ft and a length of 59ft. No 99 Sqn was again the first RAF bomber formation to receive Hinaidis in October 1929 followed again by No 10 Sqn. (via Barry Charles Wheeler)

The Handley Page Clive was a military passenger version of the Hinaidi bomber with seating for 17 troops. Two production examples were built, J9948 and J9949 and operated from 1931 by the Heavy Transport Flight at Lahore, India. They incorporated swept wings with outboard slots and two 460hp Bristol Jupiter engines which gave a maximum speed of 111mph and a range of 765 miles. (via Barry Charles Wheeler)

A potential replacement for the Fairey Fawn to Air Ministry Specification 23/25, the HP.34 Hare was a short-range, high-altitude day bomber. It flew on February 24, 1928, and afterwards survived a number of accidents, only to lose out to the Vickers Vildebeeste as the preferred choice. It later became G-ACEL before being scrapped at Hanworth in 1937. (via Barry Charles Wheeler)

Liked by its RAF crews, the W.8d Hyderabad was a heavy night bomber development of the commercial W.8 airliner and could carry 1,100lb of bombs over a 500-mile range. The first of 44 built flew in October 1923 and served with No 99 Sqn at Bircham Newton, Norfolk, and from 1928 with No 10 Sqn, seen here, at Upper Heyford. The last of the wooden-built RAF bombers, the Hyderabad was finally withdrawn from service in January 1934. (via Barry Charles Wheeler)

Possibly the greatest inter-war airliner produced in Britain, the H.P.42 became the most recognisable type of its time flown by Imperial Airways. The vast upper wing spanned 130ft and the silver, metal-skinned fuselage was 92ft in length. Inside, up to 38 passengers could view the passing scenery through wide windows along each side. On the four Bristol Jupiter engines, the aircraft cruised at 95mph, the type entering service in 1931. Production was modest, four H.P.42E or Eastern models for the Cairo, India and South African routes, and four H.P.42W or Western models for Imperial's European services. G-AAXF *Helena* was the eighth and last built. (via Barry Charles Wheeler)

In September 1938, the RAF still operated six squadrons of Heyford biplane bombers, the last converting to Whitleys in September 1939, the month war was declared. The HP.38 Heyford flew in June 1930 and 124 were produced before production ended in 1936. Slow – a maximum speed of 154mph for the Mk II – but reliable with a bomb load of 2,000lb, the Heyford was the last of the RAF's heavy biplanes. (via Barry Charles Wheeler)

A fixed-undercarriage general purpose aircraft, the H.P.47 was designed to meet three different Air Ministry requirements: replacement for the Vickers Vincent overseas; a day and night bomber to fly from unprepared aerodromes; and a land-based torpedo-bomber. The two-seat prototype K2773 flew on November 27, 1933, powered by a Bristol Pegasus III engine. Trials were undertaken at Martlesham Heath from April 1935 with further flying done at Farnborough a year later. However, time and the Air Ministry had moved on and the H.P.47 was scrapped in May 1937. (via Barry Charles Wheeler)

Built at Cricklewood and flown from Radlett on May 8, 1935, by HP test pilot Maj Codes, the H.P.51 was a monoplane conversion of the earlier unsuccessful H.P.43 biplane transport. The wing spanned 90ft and after initial trials, the Tiger engines were replaced by Bristol Pegasus IIIs and the tail modified, seen here on prototype J9833 at Farnborough in March 1937. No production order was placed for the H.P.51 and the sole example ended its days, mainly on radio trials work until scrapped in 1940. (via Barry Charles Wheeler)

A fast, manoeuvrable aircraft, the H.P.52 Hampden was the last twin-engine bomber ordered for the RAF in the expansion period before the war and against a lesser enemy than the Luftwaffe, it could have given a good account of itself. Unfortunately, it suffered serious losses on early daylight raids when its defensive armament of 0.303in guns above and below the main cabin proved wholly inadequate against the better armed German fighters. The Hampden's top speed of 245mph helped it to survive some battles and with the switch by Bomber Command to night operations, it managed to achieve some modicum of success. Production by HP, English Electric and Canadian Assn Aircraft reached 1,453. Hampdens gained later success as mine-layers and 144 were converted into torpedo-bombers.

The Hereford was developed by Short & Harland in Belfast and used the 1,000hp Napier Dagger engine in place of the Hampden's 1,000hp Bristol Pegasus radial. The first example flew with these relatively untried powerplants in October 1938, but the programme was an unhappy one with constant engine problems. The first of 100 Herefords flew in May 1939, but the type's general unserviceability saw it relegated to bomber training units.

Entering service in 1938, Hampdens were built by Handley Page and English Electric with Short Brothers in Belfast building the Napier Dagger-engined Hereford version. While the Hereford failed due to its troublesome powerplants, production of the Hampden reached 1,453 and although having a relatively sprightly performance and certainly better than that of the Wellington and Whitley, it was no match for German fighters on daylight missions, succumbing to serious losses. At night it was more survivable and became a useful minelayer, but by October 1942 the Hampden had been retired from Bomber Command. It soldiered on with Coastal Command as a torpedo-bomber, the 144 conversions giving a reasonable account of themselves against enemy shipping.

The H.P.54 Harrow, built to meet Air Ministry specification B.1/35, was ordered into production as a heavy bomber under the urgent RAF Expansion Scheme with a contract for 100 placed in 1935, but when it entered service in January 1937 it was already obsolete. While the Harrow was never employed as a bomber, it helped give RAF crews experience in handling heavy aircraft and transport conversions remained in use until 1945.

In 1936, as Britain geared once again for war, Handley Page turned its attention to a new RAF requirement for a twin-engine bomber. This would evolve into the Halifax.

Chapter 2

Halifax: The Early Years

The story of the Handley Page Halifax heavy bomber begins in the early days of the 1930s, some time before the design was committed to paper and even longer before the aircraft's exploits became headline news. Only 15 years after the end of the First World War, the British Government was once again eyeing with increasing concern Germany and its newly formed Third Reich. A huge rearmament programme was gathering pace, modern fighters and bombers began equipping a burgeoning Luftwaffe, the Wehrmacht was developing a well-armed highly mobile army, and a fleet of heavily armed warships was building for the Kriegsmarine – militarism on a grand scale was underway.

Across the North Sea, Britain had been in an age of austerity since the end of the war with armed forces more suited to policing the Empire than preparing to meet what appeared to be the hallmarks of a new totalitarian regime rising in the centre of Europe. The Royal Air Force and its leaders recognised that its outdated equipment would be woefully inadequate to meet what was emerging on the country's doorstep.

The result was the launch in 1934 of a limited rearmament programme known as Expansion Scheme A. The following year, Scheme C was adopted which called for 123 squadrons involving the replacement of biplane fighters with new monoplanes capable of more than 300mph. Innovative ideas which were new to the aviation industry would be adopted – retractable undercarriages, power-operated gun turrets, covered cockpits, etc.

On the bomber front, the biplane Handley Page Heyford, the monoplane Fairey Hendon and the HP Harrow, all with fixed spatted wheels, would be no match for what they were likely to meet in the sky over Europe. Meanwhile, work was proceeding on two new twin-engined replacements produced to Specification B.9/32, the Handley Page Hampden and the Vickers Wellington, both of which trickled into service in 1938-39. In addition, Armstrong Whitworth produced the Whitley to Spec B.3/34 for a night bomber, the first squadron forming in March 1937 when No 10 Sqn replaced its Heyfords.

Trying to create a better balanced force with adequate reserves and steer the industry towards the expected massive production increases which were to come were two men, Chief of the Air Staff Marshal of the RAF Sir Edward Ellington who took up office in 1933 and Air Marshal Wilfred Freeman, appointed Air Member for Research and Development on the Air Council on April 1, 1936. Their achievements over the expansion years cannot be overstated. They gave Britain an air force with modern, high-performance fighters which kept the Allies ahead of the enemy in capability, as well as radar and equipment to defeat the Luftwaffe in the Battle of Britain and a bomber fleet able to conduct the night war which ultimately won the battle.

Enter the Halifax

In July 1936 the Air Staff issued Specification B.12/36 and in August Spec. P.13/36 was released. The former resulted in the Short Stirling, the first of the RAF's four-engined bombers which entered service in August 1940, while from the latter in somewhat of a circuitous route came the Halifax via a twin-engined bomber proposal powered by the as yet untried 2,000hp Rolls-Royce Vulture engine.

The requirement for the P.13/36 was all-encompassing and called for an aircraft capable of dive-bombing, being catapult-launched at high weights, troop-carrying, torpedo-launching, all-round

Two pictures of the first prototype Handley Page H.P.57 Halifax, L7244. The three-quarter rear view is an official Air Ministry picture believed to have been taken at RAF Bicester after assembly following transfer from HP's factory at Cricklewood where it was built. Chief test pilot Major James Cordes first flew L7244 on October 25, 1940. The side view is another Air Ministry picture, this time taken at A&AEE Boscombe Down in November 1939 showing the wing slats which were later dispensed with on production aircraft. Lacking main wheel doors and gun turrets, the aircraft carried green and brown camouflage over all top and side areas with Night under surfaces. After A&AEE trials, the aircraft was loaned to the first operational squadron with the Halifax, No 35, for aircrew training. In 1942, it undertook trials with the Airborne Forces Experimental Establishment, before ending its flying days as a ground-based instructional airframe No 3239M. (via Barry Charles Wheeler)

Clearly identified by his trade-mark white flying suit and sporting a monocle, Major James Cordes joined Handley Page in 1928 and made the first flights of the Hyderabad, HP.42 airliner, Heyford and Hampden, before becoming closely involved in the Halifax programme. He is seen here in December 1938. Retiring at the end of the war, he died in 1980, aged 85. (*Aeroplane*)

defence using nose and tail power-operated gun turrets, and the ability to change engines on dispersal within two hours. Performance included the ability to cruise at 275mph at 15,000ft, reach a service ceiling of 28,000ft, and cover 1,000 miles with 1,000lb of bombs. The Handley Page tender was prepared by chief designer George Volkert and Reginald Stafford and submitted in March 1937. The design and performance characteristics were accepted and two prototypes were ordered in April, serialled L7244 and L7245.

The other submission was the Avro 679 Manchester, also with Vultures. By a twist of fate, this troublesome powerplant forced the withdrawal from service of the unfortunate Manchester and Avro pulled from this debacle a remarkable success when designer Roy Chadwick put forward a redesign using four Merlin XXs, which became the Avro Type 683 Manchester III, subsequently renamed Lancaster.

Meanwhile, Handley Page built a mock-up of the HP.56 at the Cricklewood works, but with the Vulture still not ready, alternative two and four-engined proposals were submitted to Air Marshal Freeman at the Air Ministry. Discussions followed, during which the dive-bombing/troop carrying/

torpedo capability and catapult take-offs were all dropped. On September 3, 1937, with the design holding promise the contract was amended from two Vultures to four Rolls-Royce Merlin Xs – thus the Halifax was born!

With serials unchanged, the two prototype HP.57s, named Halifax with Air Ministry agreement, began construction at Cricklewood in March 1938, the type supported by an initial contract for 50 Mk Is, L9485-L9534. Due to concern that Radlett's main 750-yard runway was too short for safety, it was decided that the first flight of L7244 would take place at RAF Bicester in Oxfordshire. In great secrecy the components were taken by road and assembled in a hangar and on October 25, 1939, chief test pilot Maj James Cordes took the type, undercarriage locked down, on its successful initial flight. A few days later it flew to Radlett where the second aircraft was being prepared for its transfer to the Aeroplane & Armament Experimental Establishment Boscombe Down in Wiltshire for flight trials.

Trials… and Troubles

Prototype L7244 arrived at Boscombe Down in November 1939 but flew little as minor problems emerged and were fixed by a team of HP engineers. Time on the ground was not wasted however, for various bomb combinations were loaded in to its main fuselage bay and inner wing cells to a maximum

Above and opposite: **Three views of the second Halifax prototype, L7245, taken by The Aeroplane in 1941. Thanks to the Boulton-Paul power-operated turrets in the nose and tail, the second aircraft took on a much more business-like appearance. It made its initial flight at the height of the Battle of Britain on August 17, 1940, and being close to where the Battle was taking place the precious prototype was quickly transferred to the safer airfield at Boscombe Down in Wiltshire. It retained the camouflage colours of the first aircraft, but its undersides were painted yellow to identify its experimental nature with the serial in black under each wing. The propellers were now more efficient constant-speed Rotol units, replacing the de Havilland variable-pitch airscrews on the first machine. (*Aeroplane*)**

While the prototypes were undergoing trials, Handley Page was well underway with the first production batch of Halifax B.Is of which L9485 was the first. It arrived at Boscombe Down in October 1940 and in early trials the first weaknesses of the type became apparent. Rudder overbalancing was the most serious; a problem which new crews discovered later, often to their cost. Performance too was down with the heavy turrets limiting the operational height to below the required 20,000ft and the range cut by 160 miles. L9485 undertook armament work and is shown with the bulbous Type C mid-upper fitted plus the ventral Type R. The latter was sighted using a periscope but was not adopted in service. (via Barry Charles Wheeler)

of 11,000lb, while the occasional air tests enabled stalling speeds in various configurations to be noted for the operating manuals.

At the production end of the Halifax, there was increasing urgency to get the new bomber underway and two behind the scenes events helped to meet that need. The first was prompted by a shortage of Merlin engines in the summer of 1940. Realising that 100 Merlin IIIs were sitting in France destined for the new Amiot 356 bomber, Air Marshal Freeman aimed to recover them before the Franco-German armistice on June 18. The second was the clandestine acquisition of key parts and drawings of the Messier undercarriage from the French company's factory in Paris. Messier's UK representative, Louis Armandias, was landed in southern France and made his way to the company's Paris factory where a lorry load of material was retrieved and driven down to Nice and shipped by the Royal Navy to Britain, and thence to Handley Page.

The second prototype Halifax, L7245, fitted with most of the equipment and armament planned for the production aircraft, flew at Radlett with Cordes in command on August 17, 1940, a frustrating 11 months from the first aircraft! After a few more short flights, the aircraft was flown west to the A&AEE, arriving in September 1940, followed in October by the first production Halifax B.I (L9485). Initial flight-testing indicated acceptable pilot handling, but it quickly became clear that the rudder with trim applied overbalanced at speeds below 150mph; with one or even two engines stopped on the same side, the rudder problem became acute with little chance of recovery in a turn at low altitude. This was to prove a fatal flaw in the design when the aircraft joined the squadrons.

The second aircraft succumbed to an undercarriage collapse on take-off during these early tests and repairs involved local strengthening to permit an increased take-off weight of 60,000lb. However, this extended the take-off distance by 50% and at unstick, a 'soggy' feel was experienced by the pilot as the machine staggered off the ground. Performance figures proved disappointing.

At 58,000lb the climb to 15,000ft took an extra 8 min, while the specified 20,000ft was unobtainable! Further tests showed that with full fuel and 8,000lb of bombs, the max range dropped to 1,700 miles from the expected 1,860.

Armament trials at A&AEE were mostly flown by L9485, the bulbous Type C mid-upper turret and the four-gun Type E tail turret proving workable and generally acceptable. The Type C nose turret showed slower rotation as the air speed crept above 260mph; air deflectors were fitted and improved its operation up to 310mph. In the later Mk Is, pairs of hand-operated Vickers GO beam guns were fitted in hatches and displayed no particular difficulties, apart from the exposed nature of the position for the gunners. The automatic ventral Type R turret proved troublesome with restricted views through a periscope. Gun elevation and rotation was slow and although some progress was made, the unit was mostly removed in service.

Service Entry

The first Halifax squadron, No 35 which formed part of 4 Group, was stood up at Boscombe Down on November 5, 1940, under the command of Wg Cdr RW Collings and pilot training began using L7244 which had been fitted with dual controls. Later in November, the squadron and ground echelon left for Leeming before moving in December to Linton-on-Ouse, the squadron's official operational base.

Among the early pilots was Flg Off Leonard Cheshire, the future VC holder, and rising to the challenge to assist with bringing the new bomber into service, he – and others - soon recognised that mechanically it was not ready. Typical was the hydraulic system which resulted in problems with the

Surrounded by wartime secrecy early in its career, the Halifax emerged into public view when the type was officially named by Lady Halifax at Radlett on September 12, 1941. The aircraft selected for the ceremony was L9608, the last B.I Series 3 produced and subsequently delivered to the first squadron, No 35 Sqn at Linton-on-Ouse. This much-photographed aircraft was scrapped in November 1942 when a swing on take-off collapsed the undercarriage. (*Aeroplane*)

The essence of life for a Halifax was the 1,882 gals of fuel carried on each night raid. Here, an AEC tanker pumps petrol into the tanks of a 35 Sqn aircraft. In the background sits a black-painted Armstrong Whitworth Whitley of 58 Sqn, an older resident which, in 1942 shared Linton-on-Ouse with the newer four-engine arrivals. (via Barry Charles Wheeler)

main undercarriage, while the retractable tailwheel sometimes failed to extend on landing causing minor repairs to be made to the underside of the rear fuselage. The 'archaic' fuel system also came in for criticism.

Another new arrival and a friend of Cheshire's, was Sqn Ldr JB 'Willie' Tait who became commander of A Flight in late February and was later to become one of Bomber Command's outstanding leaders. By early March, 35 Sqn had received 20 aircraft and with ten trained crews was considered ready for its first operation. The target was the heavily defended French port of Le Havre and six aircraft, led by Wg Cdr Collings, joined nine Bristol Blenheims on the night of March 10/11. They met heavy flak which peppered some of the aircraft, one experienced hydraulic failure due to battle damage, and another (L9489) was mistaken for an enemy aircraft by a British night-fighter and shot down, crashing with the loss of five men, only the pilot Sqn Ldr Gilchrist and his flight engineer managed to escape by parachute. The next night, three Halifaxes were among the 139 aircraft which attacked Hamburg.

In April, with the continuing slow delivery of new aircraft, C Flt was expanded to squadron size and formed 76 Sqn under the command of 'Willie' Tait, moving north to their new base at Middleton St George. On June 11/12, three months from the last operation due to repairs and on-going modifications, the Halifax returned to operations with a shared mission involving 76 and 35 Sqns against Duisberg, with Huls the following night. Just over a week later, on June 23/24, Bomber Command lost its first Halifax to enemy action during a raid on Kiel when L9492, one of ten Halifax taking part, piloted by P/O Stobbs from 76 Sqn was shot down by Oblt Reinhold Eckardt in a twin-engine Messerschmitt Bf 110 of II/NJG 1.

An impressive view of a 35 Sqn Halifax B.II being loaded with 500lb bombs at Linton for the upcoming night mission to Germany. As well as the main fuselage bay, bombs were also accommodated in four inner wing cells, two each side and just visible with the four ground crew members on the wing are the winches, their wires pulling the bombs into position. The windows in the side of the nose indicate the navigator's position, while at the junction of the wing and engine can be seen the balloon cable cutters. The heavy Messier undercarriage units belied their inherent weakness. (via Barry Charles Wheeler)

S-Sugar of 35 Sqn sits on a foggy, slush-covered dispersal in February 1942. It retains the second radio mast on the rear fuselage – this was deleted on later aircraft – and has darkened white areas on the roundel and fin flash. A B.II, R9441 survived until April 1943 when it crashed at Marston Moor flying with No 1652 Heavy Conversion Unit. (via Philip Jarrett)

Halifax B.II Series 1 W7676 of 35 Sqn, whose role had changed to that of Pathfinder on August 17, 1942. The aircraft was delivered in May 1942 and dispensing with the rear radio mast and now with a straight demarcation line between the camouflage and the Night black, its operational life was destructively cut short. On August 28/29, flying as a Pathfinder on a raid on Nuremberg, the crew of Sgt DA John in TL-P were part of a force of 159 bombers of which 13 were Halifaxes. The target was marked accurately, but TL-P was hit by flak and crashed in Holland with the loss of all seven crew members. (via Barry Charles Wheeler)

Flg Off Leonard Cheshire with air and ground crews in front of his 35 Sqn Halifax *Offenbach* marked with 17 mission tallies on the nose. Cheshire was one of only two Halifax pilots awarded the Victoria Cross, the other being PO Cyril Joe Barton. (via Barry Charles Wheeler)

Although production was underway, deliveries were frustratingly slow and the first 50 Halifax B.Is were followed by 25 with structural modifications to take the all-up weight from 55,000lb to the previously trialled 60,000lb. These were serialled L9560-L9584 and were designated B.I Srs 2, all fitted with additional beam guns to cover blind spots hidden from the fields of fire covered by the turrets.

Halifax Christening

Six months after the Halifax was launched on RAF operations, an official naming ceremony for the type took place at Radlett aerodrome on September 12, 1941. The obligatory bottle of champagne was smashed against the nose of Mk I L9608 with no ill-effect by Lady Halifax who, with her husband, Lord Halifax, was guest of honour at the event hosted by Mr Frederick Handley Page. A contemporary account of the day appeared in The Aeroplane in the September 19, 1941, issue, reflecting the censorship of the period.

Daylight Disasters

As 1941 moved through the early summer, the Air Staff was increasingly looking towards the use of large bombers for daylight raids. Having armed the big Halifaxes and Stirlings with power-operated turrets and in the case of the former, fitted extra defensive guns in the beam positions, Bomber Command's C-in-C Air Marshal Sir Richard Peirse was ordered to conduct what were known as 'cloud-cover raids'. If the aircraft could successfully fight their way through to the target, it was believed that it would result in greater bombing accuracy, a subject much discussed at the very highest levels of government when raid assessments in the recently compiled Butt Report showed that over 12 months nearly 49% of bombs aimed at German industrial targets actually fell in open country!

On June 30, six Halifaxes and 28 Blenheims departed mid-morning from their east coast bases and attacked a number of targets in north-west Germany, including Kiel. One Halifax, L9499 from 35 Sqn was shot down by fighters and two Blenheims were lost. The cloud masked much of the operation, but it was not too disastrous for the RAF. The next daylight mission was on July 24 when the target was the battle-cruiser *Scharnhorst* docked at La Pallice on the French west coast. Fourteen Halifaxes attacked the port, but all suffered hits and five failed to return with the loss of 16 aircrew killed and 19 taken prisoner. Five more aircraft were so seriously damaged that it took three weeks to return them to service, and a further two crew died from wounds with another 19 injured. The only consolation was that *Scharnhorst* sustained damage from five hits forcing her to remain in dock, but daylight operations were beginning to prove costly.

Design Desperations

By the end of 1941, the hope that Bomber Command would be largely re-equipped with long-range four-engined bombers – Stirlings and Halifaxes – was far from reality. The Stirling failed to gain the performance promised by Short Brothers, while the Halifax continued to be plagued by difficulties, both technical and aerodynamic, with the blame placed squarely on Handley Page.

One of the main problems with the Merlin-powered Halifax was in the engine installation. Compared with the Lancaster where Rolls-Royce advised Avro to install the Merlins well forward and below the leading edge of the wing, Handley Page positioned the Halifax nacelles higher and closer to

A moody shot of the famous 'Ruhr Valley Express' flown by No 405 (Vancouver) Sqn, RCAF. Pictured in late-1942, W7710 LQ-R carried the name on the port side of the nose, but it was short-lived as it crashed north of Flensburg – its target – on October 1/2, 1942, with the loss of all on board. (via *Aeroplane*)

No 10 Squadron was an early recipient of Halifax B.IIs and ZA-D was on a combined air test and photo-sortie with another aircraft in March 1942. (*Aeroplane*)

The urgent need for some heavy bomber support for the hard-pressed 8th Army in North Africa saw the transfer of two squadrons of Halifaxes, No 10 and 76, in the summer of 1942. They later combined to form No 462 (RAAF) Sqn. The flying view shows Z-Zebra on a familiarisation flight during the period when the bombers flew nightly 'milk-run' sorties against Tobruk. (via *Aeroplane*)

the wings, bringing the propellers nearer to the leading edge. This resulted in a higher thrust line which produced disturbed airflow over the wing, causing loss of lift, while the closeness of the propellers to the wing interfered with their efficiency causing abnormally high vibration which resulted in reduction gear failures.

When Rolls-Royce fitted Merlin 65s in Lancaster nacelles to a Halifax IV in 1943, they raised its ceiling and increased the top speed by 60mph to 324mph at 19,000ft. Unfortunately, there were insufficient two-stage Merlins available at the time, so Bristol Hercules VI and XVI radials were installed in the Halifax III and VI in longer nacelles with a lower thrust line, but the result was encouraging with at last a much-improved aircraft.

However, during the early days new crews undergoing conversion training found the Halifax B.Is particularly difficult until they mastered its idiosyncrasies. They found it difficult to taxi and the inherent swing on take-off put undue strain on the main undercarriage units leading to gear collapses. Landing meant keeping the power on during the approach, too slow could spell disaster and too fast could mean an overshoot with all that that entailed. The outboard engine radiators were susceptible to vibration which in turn lead to burst pipes and loss of coolant with the resultant rise in temperature and in some cases, engine fires.

The rudder stall problem, first encountered during handling trials at A&AEE, caught many a pilot out as he tried desperately to re-centre them to come out of a turn with 'bootfuls of force', sometimes failing with fatal results. Some of the problems were fixed by the squadrons such as the shortening of the radiator shutters. This allowed the aircraft to cruise at any height with the shutters closed instead of open; another 8mph in speed was gained. The 'elephant ear' shrouds which covered the glowing engine exhausts on either side of the cowlings were considered by pilots to reduce performance and increase turbulence, so despite their signature brightness to prowling night-fighters the ground crews removed them and sure enough, performance went up and surprisingly, losses went down! Handley Page subsequently designed an improved lightweight engine shroud which took in ideas from the squadrons.

Another element that degraded performance was the surface friction of the matt camouflage paint. While some squadrons applied a semi-matt finish, Handley Page engineers again listened to the

Halifax W1253 of 158 Sqn managed to reach home waters from a raid on Genoa on November 7/8, 1942, but the fuel ran out heading for its base at Rufforth and P/O Beveridge put the dead-engined aircraft down in the River Humber. Sadly three members of the crew died in the ditching. (via Philip Jarrett)

users and soon aircraft were being delivered in the smoother covering, adding a precious 5mph to the cruise speed.

Some enterprising pilots on 76 Sqn, urged on by the later CO, Sqn Ldr Cheshire, gained more height and speed by taking out all excess weight, including sections of interior armour plate. The aircraft's early period in service brought much adverse criticism, one pilot commenting that 'it remained a lumbering, under-powered sitting target'.

The same, but different

The first Halifax B.II, designated HP.59, was flown by Cordes at Radlett on July 3, 1941, followed two months later by the first production example, L9609 which went to 76 Sqn. It looked almost identical to the B.I but incorporated 1,390hp Merlin XX engines, larger oil coolers, increased fuel to 1,882 Imp gal and a Boulton-Paul mid-upper turret mounting two 0.303s replacing the earlier beam guns. Modified jigs and tooling were passed to the London Aircraft Production Group which built 450 at Leavesden, Rootes Securities at Speke which built 12 and English Electric at Samlesbury where 900 would be completed; Handley Page produced 615.

In a similar fashion to the B.I, the revamped B.II still couldn't improve on performance so after a short spell on operations, the Mk II Series 1 Special appeared. This did away with the nose turret, replaced with a solid 'Z-fairing'; the large mid-upper turret was removed as were the exhaust muffs. Refining the result, Handley Page produced the Mk II Series 1A which introduced the longer, moulded Perspex nose which increased the overall length by 22in to a new standard of 71ft 7in. A smaller, Defiant-like four-gun mid-upper turret was fitted, and redesigned engine cowlings now covered the 1,390hp Merlin XXIIs. The result was a 20mph increase in cruising speed. The final change brought large, near rectangular fins which served to dampen yaw effects and improve bombing accuracy.

The Halifax undercarriage and the associated hydraulics problem refused to go away and the French-designed Messier gear continued to give trouble. To find a cure, Dowty was approached and proposed a new levered-suspension system similar to that fitted to the Lancaster. This proved marginally successful, but the call on undercarriage production meant that the Halifax would have to continue with both the Messier unit and the new Dowty system. To identify the two differently-equipped aircraft, Halifax B.IIs fitted with the latter units became B.Vs. These were built only by Rootes Securities at Speke and Fairey Aviation at Stockport. Production of the Mk V ended in January 1944 after 904 had been delivered.

The first Halifax B.II lost on operations was L9612 and came not from a mainline bomber squadron but from the secretive 138 Special Duty Sqn based at Newmarket. It had been conducting a sortie over Poland and put down at Tormelilla in Sweden early on the morning of November 2, 1941, reportedly low on fuel. The four Polish crew members set fire to the aircraft and eventually returned to England.

At the end of a year during which Bomber Command had failed to make any real impression on raiding Germany, the Air Staff remained convinced that daylight operations had their place in the overall bombing plan. The target for the mid-morning attack on Brest on December 18 was once again the German battlecruisers, *Scharnhorst* and *Gneisenau* or 'Salmon and Gluckstein' as they were widely known in Britain. The force of 47 aircraft comprised 18 Stirlings and 11 Manchesters, plus 18 Halifaxes from the recently re-equipped 10 Sqn at Leeming as well as from 35 and 76 Sqns. They bombed from 16,000ft with Spitfires giving cover, but six bombers were lost of which one Halifax B.II (V9978) was forced to ditch. It was that of the 35 Sqn CO Wg Cdr Basil Robinson DFC; fortunately, all the crew survived and returned to Linton.

While it looked convincing to the crews, the attack failed to dent the two ships, so a further daylight raid was ordered and on December 30, 18 Halifaxes from the same three squadrons were mustered.

Aircraft and photographer cast long shadows in the early morning sunrise. The abrasive nature of desert sand is clearly evident on the engines and wing of a 76 Sqn Halifax and much work was needed from the ground crews to keep machines operational in such extreme conditions. With little opposition from fighters on the night raids, guns were removed from the nose turrets and the gaps filled in, seen on the aircraft in the background. (via *Aeroplane*)

Fourteen finally bombed, but despite Spitfire cover three aircraft were lost, one from each squadron, of which only one crew survived. Again, damage to the ships was minimal. Some five weeks later, the two German warships, accompanied by the cruiser *Prinz Eugen*, sailed from Brest and made the infamous dash through the English Channel in a carefully planned operation. A frantic response by British forces included 242 sorties by Bomber Command within which 13 Halifaxes took part, but low cloud and driving rain frustrated attempts to locate the ships and amidst national humiliation in Britain, they reached Germany almost unscathed.

Command change and Halifax progress

Of more importance than the desultory missions made by Britain's bomber force through to the end of 1941 was the change in leadership which took place on January 8, 1942, when Bomber Command C-in-C AM Sir Richard Pierse, judged responsible by the Air Staff for poor results combined with increasing losses in men and aircraft, was posted to the Far East.

A new policy decided that area bombing would be the only way to defeat Nazi Germany and a suggested force of no fewer than 4,000 bombers would be needed to undertake the task. However, such a figure called for huge resources from the industry while the RAF would require 250 high calibre squadron commanders as well as 750 good flight commanders, considered by some to be an impossible goal. With the policy came a new leader for Bomber Command, Air Chief Marshal Sir Arthur Harris who took over on February 22, 1942, and from that inspired appointment came the eventual forging of the British strategic bomber force which destroyed much of Germany's war machinery and laid waste to its cities.

A measure of the huge problem confronting Harris when he took over to implement the new policy was a paltry force of 378 serviceable aircraft of which 69 were heavy bombers. Amidst all the gloom, Harris also had to relinquish some of his precious Halifaxes in order to save the rapidly deteriorating situation in North Africa where Field Marshal Erwin Rommel was pushing the Allied armies back towards Egypt.

However, before that, Bomber Command managed three noteworthy operations. The first took place on the night of March 3/4, 1942, and was the largest raid of the war to date, when 235 aircraft of which only 20 were Halifaxes, successfully bombed the Renault factory at Boulogne-Billancourt near Paris. Led by experienced crews who attacked the target accurately and from a lower-than-normal altitude, the force devastated 40% of the buildings stopping vehicle production for four weeks. Just a single Wellington was lost.

The second operation was an attempt to sink or severely damage the *Tirpitz* battleship which was moored in Trondheim Fjord in Norway. On April 27, 1942, a force of 31 Halifaxes and 12 Lancasters took off and duly found the ship, but despite dropping 1,000lb spherical mines designed to sink and explode under the ship thereby rupturing the hull, the attack failed and six Halifaxes and a Lancaster were lost. One of the former was W1048 of 35 Sqn flown by P/O MacIntyre. Hit by flak which started a fire in the starboard wing, MacIntyre skilfully crash-landed on the nearby frozen lake near Hocklingen.

A ferry flight which went wrong! Halifax B.II W7756 of 462 Sqn was landing at El Daba on November 28, 1942, when it stalled on landing, collapsing the undercarriage and breaking the aircraft's back. No casualties – but drinks in the bar were on the pilot, Sgt Gibbons RAAF! (via Philip Jarrett)

Its flaps lowered, Halifax B.II BB339 of 178 Sqn lands at Fayid, Egypt, on April 17, 1943. 'P-Peter' was one of the force of heavy bombers tasked with raids on targets in Sicily, Crete, Italy and the Aegean islands. (via *Aeroplane*)

The crew survived, all but one evading capture, and the aircraft sank below the surface. Thirty-one years later, the wreck was raised and brought back to England and placed on display in the RAF Museum, Hendon (see story, page 124).

The third operation was on May 30/31 when Halifaxes took part in the RAF's first 1,000-bomber raid on Germany. Harris initially chose Hamburg, the second largest city in Germany, as the target, but poor weather forced a change to Cologne. The force comprised 1,047 aircraft cobbled together from 1, 3, 4 and 5 Groups, plus aircraft from 91 and 92 (OTU) Groups as well as Flying Training Command. Of the 131 Halifaxes despatched from the front-line and training units, three were lost of the 41 aircraft of all types listed as missing. The consoling fact for the Air Staff was the enormous damage done to property and industrial firms across the city from the 1,455 tons of bombs and incendiaries dropped, while for a hard-pressed Britain it proved a huge propaganda coup. Essen received the same treatment the following night, on June 1/2, but results were nowhere near as dramatic and of the 31 bombers lost, eight were Halifaxes. Area bombing had come to the Third Reich!

Down to the Desert

On June 22, 1942, the day after Tobruk fell to Rommel's Afrika Korps with the surrender of its garrison of 25,000 men, two detachments of 16 Halifaxes each from 10 and 76 Sqns were ordered to fly out to Aqir in Palestine to help shore-up the retreating Allied armies. These aircraft formed 462 (RAAF)

Sqn within No 249 Wing and under 205 Group and were supported by a force of US Army Air Force Consolidated B-24D Liberators requested urgently by Churchill from President Roosevelt.

The hastily transferred Halifax II crews mounted their first raid, unsurprisingly against Tobruk, on July 11/12 and the enemy-held coastal town became a regular target thereafter. Although the unit suffered the usual Halifax woes connected with the hydraulics and a lack of sufficient spares in a particularly punishing environment, it was not until the night of September 5/6 that the force lost its first aircraft during an attack on the enemy transport base at Heraklion, Crete. Flt Lt Bryan piloting W1144 was shot down and killed, together with another member of the crew, by Feldwebel Liebhold of III/JG 27 flying a Bf 109 fighter; the other five crew members became PoWs.

Although the Halifax detachment was only due to last 16 days, the type remained in the Mediterranean for the remainder of the war, moving from Fayid in the Canal Zone to El Adem in Libya until January 1944 when the squadron transferred to the Italian mainland. It was subsequently renumbered 614 (RAF) Sqn and undertook a Pathfinding and target marking role for the squadrons operating within No 205 Group.

It was while based at Cellone, near Foggia, that the squadron received its first B.IIs equipped with Gee, H2S 360º search radar and the later Mk 14 bombsight. These improvements gave the Halifax force greater capability on its wide-ranging attacks against enemy oil targets as well as marshalling yards, airfields, bridges and troop concentrations. The final operation by a Halifax Pathfinder based in Italy was against an oil depot on March 3, 1945.

Halifax Squadrons, RAF Bomber Command, January 1942			
No 4 Group	10 Sqn	Leeming	17 a/c
	35 Sqn	Linton-on-Ouse	19 a/c
	76 Sqn	Middleton St George	12 a/c

Chapter 3

Halifax:
The Middle Years

By the spring of 1942, seven squadrons of No 4 Group in Yorkshire were flying Halifaxes (10, 35, 76, 78, 102, 158, and 405) and despite its technical drawbacks operations with the type finally began to gather pace. In addition to airframe assembly at Handley Page's Cricklewood and Radlett factories, production was ramping up at four other locations; English Electric at Preston, Rootes at Speke, Fairey at Stockport and the London Aircraft Production Group which involved the London

Removing the rarely-used nose turret to save weight and replacing it with a so-called 'Z' fairing was a modification the early Halifaxes underwent from early 1942. Three such aircraft are seen at English Electric's factory having received the change to become B.II Series 1 (Special) versions. In the centre, W1173 carries the markings of 405 (Vancouver) Sqn, RCAF, having originally served with 35 Sqn following delivery in mid-1942. LQ-X still carries the Boulton-Paul Type C turret while JB929 in the background has the later raised and faired four-gun Defiant-type B-P Type A turret. Both aircraft survived enemy action, only to succumb to the bet noir of the type, undercarriage collapses! (via Mike Hooks)

Passenger Transport Board with its numerous sites and depots across the capital. Feeding these centres were 600 sub-contractors employing 51,000 people supplying the thousands of parts which made up each bomber. By the end of 1942, aircraft manufacture was the largest single industry in Britain, employing over 1,650,000 people, run by the Ministry of Aircraft Production under the astute and experienced control of Chief Executive ACM Sir Wilfrid Freeman.

Major components such as the Merlin engines were flowing from Rolls-Royce, gun turrets from Boulton Paul, undercarriages from Messier and Dowty, tyres from Dunlop, and propellers from Rotol. In the peak period, a total of 41 factories and dispersal units were involved in Halifax production and one aircraft was completed each working hour. English Electric, for instance, produced more Halifaxes than any other contractor, building two aircraft per day in md-1943 towards its final total of 2,145.

To maintain conformity and accuracy in production, one aircraft from every hundred produced by the main contractors was flown down to Radlett where it was inspected, and test flown. Any deficiencies discovered by the Handley Page engineers and pilots were notified to the firm concerned and remedial action quickly taken.

Architect of the Allied night-bombing strategy, Air Chief Marshal Sir Arthur Harris. Loved by his 'boys', he was undoubtedly 'the right man at the right time' to prosecute the destruction of Hitler's war machine. (via _Aeroplane_)

Criticism from the Top

Nevertheless, by August 1942 both the Stirling and the Halifax were causing increasing concern for the head of Bomber Command, ACM Sir Arthur Harris. To co-ordinate effective raids, the key was in aircraft performance, but Harris had inherited a force of mismatched bombers. At the top of the performance curve was the Lancaster which exceeded its specification and could carry 8,000lb of bombs to Berlin at heights between 22,000 and 27,000ft at cruising speeds of around 240mph. Against these figures, the Stirling was hard put to cruise at a little over 200mph at only 14,000ft, while the Halifax struggled to 18,000ft, making both more vulnerable to flak.

Harris' frustration boiled over in December 1942 prompting a letter to the Secretary of State for Air, Sir Archibald Sinclair, in which he commented that he welcomed the cessation of Stirling production as 'they make no worth…in return for their overheads. I am lucky if I can raise 30 Stirlings from 3 Group for one night's work after a week of doing nothing [due to weather], or 20 the night after.'

'Much the same applies to the Halifax issue…nothing is being done to make this deplorable product worthy for war… [or for] our gallant crews. Unless we can get these two vital factors…put right, and with miraculous despatch, we are sunk. In Russia it would long ago have been arranged with a gun, and to that extent I am a fervid Communist!'

Harris made clear that he wanted all bomber production to centre on the Lancaster, but the switch for the industry was nigh on impossible if a strategic bombing campaign was to start in short-order and while the Stirling Production Group took on the Avro-designed bomber, the enormous investment and resources involving the large-scale assembly of Halifaxes meant cancellation was not a practical option. On the positive side, hope was being pinned on aircraft receiving new equipment to increase bombing accuracy, a subject which had come in for much heated criticism.

Gee, H2S and Oboe

A new radio-based navigation system known a Gee appeared in late 1941 and used interrelated VHF pulses transmitted from ground stations, the aircraft position being determined by observing intervals between pulses from pairs of stations and plotting them on a map. It would 'home' aircraft back to their bases after raids but would not provide blanket accuracy for bombing in bad weather. In the see-saw world of early electronics, it was not long before the Germans learned about Gee and jammed it, turning the radar screen into 'grass' to prevent a reading.

The second new aid was also originally intended for navigation but turned out to be the answer to the question of bombing accuracy. This was H2S, a centimetric-wavelength radar which scanned the ground below the aircraft, returning echoes on a cathode-ray tube which indicated by strength of picture whether the area over which the aircraft was flying was built-up, such as a town which gave a strong signal, countryside which produced a weaker signal, or water which was weakest of all.

Developed by the Telecommunications Research Establishment (TRE) at Swanage, the new radar, identified by the large ventral bulge housing the scanner, was first installed in Halifax V9977 on January 4, 1942, trials beginning at Hurn on April 16. Unfortunately, on June 7 the aircraft sustained an engine fire and crashed near Ross-on-Wye with the loss of the crew and five scientists. The urgent testing of the H2S radar continued with B.II W7711.

Third was Oboe, a blind-bombing system which used two ground stations and a pulse repeater in the aircraft to guide the crew to the desired release point with unerring accuracy, around 150 yards was average. It could not be jammed and allowed specialist PFF Mosquitoes in particular to mark the targets more precisely; it came into service in January 1943.

By mid-1942, the Halifax was taking on more of Bomber Command's main operations and on June 25/26 Bremen was the target for another 1,000-bomber raid of which 124 were Halifaxes. Less

With the last glimmer of daylight disappearing in the west, a 77 Sqn Halifax B.II Series 1 (Special) gathers speed on take-off from Elvington for another raid on the Ruhr in June 1943. The squadron had converted to Halifaxes in October 1942 and retained the type until the end of the war. (via *Aeroplane*)

Proving it could maintain height on two engines, Halifax B.II Series 1 (Special) BB324 carried the name 'Haig's for Victory' together with four sortie markings on the other side of the nose. As well as the fairing where the mid-upper turret was previously located, this view also shows the breather on the upper surface of the wing for the two fuel tanks between the engines and a further breather near the outer wing roundels. This aircraft was lost off the Dutch coast with Sgt Pinkerton's crew on a raid against Mulheim on June 22/23, 1943. (via Barry Charles Wheeler)

spectacular than the big Cologne attack, the results were more damaging to the German industry with shipyards and a refinery being hit, while at the Focke-Wulf factory an assembly shop was flattened by a single 4,000lb bomb. Unfortunately, RAF losses were grim, 48 aircraft failed to return of which nine were Halifaxes. This was 5% of the force and the largest loss suffered by the Command to date.

Path Finder Force Established

The idea of a specialist target finding force to lead the main bomber streams was first endorsed in 1941 by the then Deputy Director of Bomber Operations, Gp Capt Sydney Bufton. When put to Harris, he condemned the idea as elitist and responded that to strip the best crews from the squadrons would result in a mediocre force with no encouragement and inspiration for new crews. The argument against the idea of 'crack' squadrons was supported through the upper echelons of the RAF, including among the Bomber Group Commanders, and persisted through the summer of 1942 until the Chief of the Air Staff, Sir Charles Portal, supported by Churchill, ordered Harris to prepare for the formation of the new force.

Thus, on August 15 the Path Finder Force (PFF) was established under the command of Australian Wg Cdr Don Bennett, a former Halifax squadron CO within No 4 Group. Five squadrons formed

All trades found themselves the subject of group photographs sometime during their tours of duty, in this case Wireless Operators flying with 158 Sqn at Rufforth. Front row left to right: Flt Sgt MacKie, Sgt Carstairs, Flt Sgt Rowsell RCAF, Flg Off Winship, Sgt Brown, Sgt Duffy, Flt Sgt Koch RCAF, and Flt Sgt Morgan RCAF. Behind stand five members of the ground-crew who probably looked after the B.II Series 1 (Special) behind. (via Barry Charles Wheeler)

the new Pathfinders, one from each of the Groups; 156 Sqn (Wellingtons) from No 1 Gp, 109 Sqn (Wellingtons and Mosquitoes) from 2 Gp, 7 Sqn (Stirlings) from 3 Gp, 35 Sqn (Halifaxes) from 4 Gp and 83 Sqn (Lancasters) from 5 Gp. Their bases were in Huntingdonshire and Cambridgeshire, namely Oakington, Graveley, Wyton and Warboys.

To mark the targets, new flares and special-coloured indicators were designed, but the new role was more than just a matter of dropping a few coloured lights. Firstly, in order not to dazzle the following bomb aimers, hooded flares were devised to illuminate the target. Secondly, the Target Indicators themselves were of varying weights from 250lb up to 1,000lb. They fell like ordinary bombs until they reached a predetermined height, usually 3,000ft, where they explosively ejected 60 brilliantly coloured pyrotechnic candles which spread as they fell to form a distinctive pool of fire some 300 yards in diameter. Marking the target called for a high standard of accuracy from the whole crew, but mainly the pilot, bomb aimer and navigator in order that the red, green or yellow TIs were dropped in exactly the right place, either on the ground or in the air above. The biggest problem was smoke and when this obscured the target, additional markers were deliberately dropped offset to the main aiming point and the Main Force were given a false wind to be set on their bombsights. With this, they aimed at the markers and if they had been dropped accurately, the bombs would fall on the target.

From mid-1943, a so-called 'master of ceremonies' accompanied the raid as Master Bomber. Flown by an experienced crew, the aircraft was one of the first to arrive in the vicinity of the target and directed the attack, advising the Main Force by VHF R/T of any changes to the plan, such as moving the aiming point below to a different part of the target and/or requesting PFF bombers to drop coloured TIs in a different area to maximise damage. Flying as Master Bomber was a particularly hazardous task as he remained over the target until all the Main Force had dropped their bombs.

In January 1943, the PFF became a separate group, No 8, and on the night of the 16/17th flew its first operational mission with TIs on a Berlin raid, incidentally, also the first use of an all four-engined bombing force from which Stirlings had been withdrawn. Mainly a No 5 Group operation, the force comprised 190 Lancasters and 11 Halifaxes, but the result was only partially successful, haze over the city obscuring targets, although encouragingly for such a deep penetration flight over enemy territory, losses amounted to only one Lancaster.

Solving problems with later marks

While Bomber Command planners continued to try to integrate the poor performance of the early Halifaxes into their calculations for the nightly raids, Handley Page designers were still working hard at trying to eliminate or at least reduce the type's weaknesses. As noted previously, from December 1941 the front and mid-upper turrets had been removed and a new nose fairing fitted under Mod.398, saving 1,500lb in weight, resulting in the Halifax Mk II Series 1 (Special); the triple fuel jettison pipes were also removed from beneath each wing.

In August 1942 a more refined transparent nose was produced under Mod.452. Approved in December '42, aircraft so fitted became Mk II Series 1a versions and somewhat defeating the whole

The remains of DK148 *Johnnie the Wolf* at Holme-on-Spalding Moor after Flt Lt Shannon RAAF had coaxed the already damaged aircraft across Germany to a crash-landing at its base following a raid on Essen on July 25/26, 1943. Flying its 15th sortie, the aircraft lost its port inner propeller which struck the fuselage. Losing control, the pilot gave the order to bale out, but only the mid-upper gunner did so before Shannon righted the aircraft and with the other five crew members still aboard flew the aircraft home. Two weeks later, on August 9, Shannon with a well-earned DFC and his crew were shot down in flames by flak in Halifax B.V LK892 returning from Mannheim. (via Barry Charles Wheeler)

The Halifax B.II Series 1a was the next version to see service. Identified by the transparent nose combined with Merlin engines, these examples were at HP's Radlett airfield awaiting delivery early in 1943. Still with a weighty mid-upper turret, performance remained below requirements. (*Flight*)

idea of the change, initial aircraft received a four-gun Boulton Paul dorsal turret. Up went the weight again to 60,000lb and in this configuration the Series 1a could only take around 2,000lb of bombs to Berlin. The slender bomb bay was not suited to the larger weapons being introduced so to accommodate the later 4,000lb 'Cookie', new enlarged doors were designed, while for the 8,000lb 'Super Cookie' (two 4,000lb explosive cylinders bolted together), an enlarged fairing was developed to encase the weapon. The first of these monsters was dropped from a 76 Sqn Halifax during an attack on Essen on April 10/11, 1942; the result is unknown!

Halifax B.III and VI – the First with Radials

The long-discussed adoption of Bristol Hercules radial engines, first requested by Air Marshal FJ Linnell, Controller Research and Development, in September 1941, at last became a reality the following year. A previously low-priority development, the plan was hastened towards a prototype with Mk II Series 1 (Special) R9534 making its initial flight as the HP.61 with 1,615hp Hercules VIs on October 12, 1942. Structural modifications, such as the almost rectangular fins and rudders – known as 'D' fins – raised the all-up weight to 64,000lb, but the speed was estimated at 307mph at 31,000ft! However, operational figures came down to a more realistic 282mph with a ceiling of 24,000ft.

The MAP ordered what was designated the Halifax Mk III into production in February 1943 and the first example of what would be the best of the breed flew on August 29, 1943, with initial deliveries in November to No 433 Sqn, RCAF, and 466 Sqn, RAAF. More Halifax IIIs were built than any other variant, a total of 2,127 rolling off the production lines and equipping 41 operational squadrons. To increase operating height, all but the first few Mk IIIs and the later B.VI with 1,675hp Hercules 100s incorporated an increased wing span with rounded tips from the previous 98ft 10in to 104ft 2in. Another refinement was a retractable tailwheel which had previously been fixed down because of its

Handley Page's test aircraft for the rounded transparent nose and extended inner nacelle was L9515, seen at Radlett in 1943. The longer low-drag nose provided a sitting position for the bomb-aimer as well as more stowage space. (*Flight*)

Despite losing the complete port inner engine and damaging the outer propeller in the process, *The Wizard of Oz* limped back to its base at Pocklington after the raid on Kassel on October 3, 1943. The 102 Sqn B.II Series 1A was commanded by Australian Flt Sgt McPhail. (via Barry Charles Wheeler)

unreliability and troublesome shimmy on the ground during taxiing. The bomb load was now 10,000lb in the fuselage bay with an additional 3,000lb in the inner wing bays. Fuel capacity was raised to 2,688gal, a major increase from the 1,392gal carried by the B.I and II.

As deliveries began, training on the new version commenced and it fell to HX237 of 466 Sqn to be the first of its type to succumb to the still problematical undercarriage weakness. On take-off at Leconfield, it swung and collapsed, the damage being too severe for repair; it had just 26.10 flying hours logged.

The B.VI was similar to the Mk III, but incorporated a revised fuel system for tropical operations. The prototype flew on December 19, 1943, but it was ten months before the first production example left the ground on October 10, 1944. Production totalled 132 by HP and 325 by English Electric. With a gross weight of 68,000lb, the B.VI climbed to 20,000ft in 50min, after which it could cruise at around 220mph for 1,260 miles carrying full fuel and bombs.

Target – Germany and Ruhr

By the beginning of 1943, Bomber Command continued to be the only force capable of striking at the heart of Germany. The Americans started bombing targets across the Channel in daylight, but it would be some time before the United States Army Air Force would have the numbers of aircraft capable of carrying the war to the enemy heartland. Harris' bombers were to conduct what the Allies had formulated at the January Casablanca Conference '…the progressive destruction and dislocation of the German military, industrial and economic system, and the undermining of the morale of the German people to a point where their capacity for armed resistance is fatally weakened.'

A line of weather-beaten target marking B.II Series 1 (Specials) of No 614 Sqn in the final stages of the North African war in 1943. The 'veteran' K-King in the foreground exhibits 45 missions on the nose. (via Philip Jarrett)

In the hope that later Halifaxes would make use of the newer and more powerful Rolls-Royce Merlin 60 series two-stage engine to create the B.IV, Handley Page built and tested Halifax B.II Series 2 HR756. With four-blade propellers and extended inner nacelles, the trials aircraft was flown as a test bed in March 1943 and with supercharged 65s it raised its ceiling and increased its speed by 60mph to 324mph at 19,000ft. However, HP was told there were not enough two-stage Merlins to go round and the Bristol Hercules radial would power subsequent Halifax marks. (via Barry Charles Wheeler)

After its hesitatingly poor start, the Halifax was beginning to show what it could do. No 35 Sqn was now part of the PFF and ten Halifaxes were fitted with H2S to give the raids an accuracy which had long been wanted. Three-quarters of the aircraft in No 4 Group were now Halifaxes and several hundred four-engined bombers could be launched in answer to the Allied dictum. First off, however, were the U-Boat bases along the French west coast in an attempt to reduce the effectiveness of the submarines attacking Atlantic convoys. This was much against Harris' plans for his force, but Churchill insisted that the enormous losses in merchant ships and their vital cargoes must be curbed. Lorient was first on January 14/15 when 122 aircraft bombed the port, 63 Halifaxes taking part, followed by a second raid the next night by 157 aircraft of which 48 were Halifaxes. St Nazaire was attacked through February, March and April.

Berlin was raided on January 16/17, 1943, and again the next night, but three Halifaxes and 19 Lancasters were shot down, 11.8% of the force. In a quirk of fortune, the raid on Berlin on March 1/2 by 302 aircraft, of which 86 were Halifaxes, resulted in damage to the Telefunken radar factory. Destroyed was the first H2S radar set obtained by the Germans from a shot down Stirling near Rotterdam, and which was being reassembled for technical assessment. However, the British success was short-lived as a 35 Sqn Halifax B.II – believed to be W7877 flown by Sqn Ldr P Elliott DFC – was lost on this night over Holland presenting the enemy with an almost intact replacement for the set lost earlier!

Through April, Bomber Command attacked towns supplying Hitler's war machine, Essen, Duisburg, Mannheim, Pilsen and Stettin. Three, four and five hundred aircraft thundered across the North Sea nightly and at last, the Halifax was appearing in numbers nearing those despatched by the Lancaster-equipped squadrons. But as the Halifax numbers increased, so the losses mounted.

To trial the four Bristol Hercules VI engines and the new fin and rudder shape, Mk II Series 1 (Special) R9534 was duly modified and given daylight camouflage and yellow undersurfaces. The rectangular fins and rudders finally fixed the rudder lock-over problem. (via Barry Charles Wheeler)

Dortmund on May 23/24 was a case in point. A heavy raid by 826 bombers including 199 Halifaxes and 343 Lancasters, against this Ruhr target proved successful with 2,000 buildings destroyed and the large Hoesch steelworks hit badly enough to halt production. On the debit side was the loss of 18 Halifax aircraft, eight of which were known to have been shot down by the increasingly effective Luftwaffe night-fighter force; the others were hit by flak or disappeared in unknown circumstances. Ten more Halifaxes were lost on the May 27/28 Essen attack, 16 more on the June 11/12 raid on Dusseldorf (of a total of 38 aircraft in total), and 11 on the 28/29 attack on Cologne. When the Battle of the Ruhr ceased in early July, over 200 Halifaxes had been lost within No 4 Group alone in the 18-week campaign. Hamburg and Berlin were to follow.

As well as bombing raids, minelaying missions, known as Gardening operations, were flown, but the work of laying mines was no less dangerous. One example was the operation on April 28/29, 1943, when 60 Halifax IIs joined 147 Lancasters, Stirlings and Wellingtons, on flights off Heligoland and over the River Elbe. A total of 593 mines were dropped, the largest number to date, but AA fire and nightfighters claimed 22 aircraft, including two Halifaxes, one from 158 Sqn at Lissett and the other from 419 Sqn at Middleton St George. Aircrew losses for that one operation totalled 145 killed with just four surviving as PoWs.

Hamburg…

By the summer of 1943, the northern city of Hamburg had been attacked 98 times since the start of the War. It was Europe's largest port and Germany's second largest city, putting it very near the top of Bomber Command's target list when Harris ordered a series of raids against this sprawling home of 1.75 million people. The first raid was on the night of July 24/25 when 791 aircraft, including 246 Halifaxes, bombed the centre of the city.

Of the 12 aircraft lost, only four were Halifaxes and the low casualty figure – only 1.5% of the force – was due mainly to the first use of Window by the RAF. These strips of coarse black paper, 27cm long and 2cm wide with thin aluminium foil on one side of the strip produced false echoes on the German Wurzburg early-warning radars, also on the smaller Lichtenstein radars used by the night-fighters and on the searchlight system. Their screens were rendered useless, preventing any chance of tracking the bombers and blinding the systems used by the airborne radar observers.

Two nights later, a similar number of bombers, 787 of which 729 dropped 2,326 tons of bombs on the city, repeated the earlier attack, but this time a hellish firestorm developed which consumed everything in a densely built-up area. It raged for some three hours and killed approximately 40,000 people. Two more raids and daylight attacks by the US 8th Air Force on the city contributed to its further destruction and forced much of the population to flee in to the countryside. The widespread savagery of the bombing also prompted first comments in some German circles that the war was lost. Meanwhile, Bomber Command moved to its next major campaign.

...and Berlin

The Nazi seat of government and the capital of the Third Reich, Berlin had been attacked a number of times, first on August 25/26, 1940, and later with increasing numbers of bombers. Taking on the 1,150-mile round trip on August 23/24, 1943, produced another 'first' for Harris's stoic crews when 56 aircraft failed to return from 727 dispatched – 7.9% of the force and the greatest loss for the Command to date! The Halifax fared badly compared with the Lancaster with 23 lost against 17 respectively, one of the four Mk IIs lost from No 35 Sqn taking the new Graveley Station Commander, the experienced Gp Capt Robinson DSO DFC, to his death. Damage was done to a number of districts, but aircrew casualties would portend worse to come.

November 18, 1943, was the 'official' start of the Berlin Campaign and it also heralded the final withdrawal of the Short Stirling from Bomber Command's main force. This 1930s design was now too slow and vulnerable, 109 Stirlings failing to return from raids between August and November, a 6.9% loss rate. This left the Halifax and Lancaster to take on the German defences. The first raid of the planned pulverising of the Nazi capital saw just nine losses, an encouraging beginning but as the plan expanded, things changed.

Harris never concealed his strong preference for the Lancaster over what he considered was the weaker and undesirable Halifax and had ordered that the former should take on the lion's share of the Berlin operation, a fact highlighted on the September 3/4 mission which was an all-Lancaster affair with 316 taking part of which 22 were lost.

Between November and January 1944, Berlin was attacked nine times and in that first month of 1944, the Command lost no fewer than 314 aircraft to flak and fighters on night operations with a further 416 returning damaged of which 38 were 'damaged beyond economical repair'. In fact, the statistics tell a gloomy tale which for many observers and historians, showed clearly that Harris and Bomber Command had lost the Battle of Berlin.

Typical of the casualties were the figures for the January 20/21 raid by 769 aircraft. Thirty-five were lost (22 Halifaxes of which five were from No 102 Sqn at Pocklington), eclipsed by those on the January 28/29 mission when 46 aircraft (26 Halifaxes) were shot down, followed by the large February 15/16 attack by 891 bombers when 43 aircraft failed to return (17 Halifaxes from a force of over 300 deployed for the first time), and the last against the capital on March 24/25 which resulted in 72 losses out of 810 or 8.88% (28 Halifaxes). Lumped in with these brave efforts were raids on Leipzig and Nuremburg, the latter seeing 95 bombers fall to the enemy of which 31 were Halifaxes from a total force of 795 – a shattering 11.94% and the largest loss of the war. From these two raids alone, nearly 1,000 aircrew would not return to their airfields in Britain.

In spite of huge swathes of Berlin now in ruins, including much of Hitler's Government area, the RAF could not sustain the losses in men and machines. Between November 1943 and March 1944, 1,117 aircraft had been lost and 1,682 damaged. The hoped-for collapse of morale and the destruction of German industry remained unachieved, in fact production increased as factories were more widely dispersed and the blind dedication to the Fuhrer by the German population continued undiminished.

Hazards in the Air

Group Captain Tom Sawyer DFC was a Halifax pilot and later station commander of a Halifax base in No 4 Group. He remembers some of the problems that were encountered during the mid-war period.

'By 1943, the Halifax II had become somewhat unsatisfactory as far as those who had to fly them were concerned. The extra equipment we had to carry – Gee, H2S, radar jamming device against night fighters, more fuel and higher bomb loads, etc, were all adding weight to our aeroplanes which the original Merlin engines were now too underpowered to cope with.

'All these combined to reduce our operational height, and consequently we were always flying well below the Lancasters and receiving more than our fair share of attention from enemy flak and fighters. This was showing up in that the loss rate of Halifaxes ran at a higher percentage than the Lancs at that time. Our Halibags were also being showered with incendiaries from the Lancasters on occasions, pattering heavily all over our aeroplanes in a most unwelcome manner. Add to this the occasional bomb suddenly arriving inside the fuselage from above, and the resultant alarm and despondency caused to the crews on the receiving end can readily be imagined.

'One Halifax crew came back one night having received a heavy calibre bomb which entered the top of the fuselage just aft of the mid-upper turret, much to the indignation of the gunner, and which carried on straight through the aeroplane leaving a gaping hole at the port wing root. The pilot, Flt Sgt Cameron, flew his crippled bomber back to base and made a safe landing after a somewhat draughty and uncomfortable return flight. Another Halifax reported having a 500lb bomb suddenly appearing through the roof and remain lying about inside the fuselage. Two of the crew had to open a side hatch and roll the thing out.'

Halifax Squadrons, RAF Bomber Command, March 1943			
No 4 Group	10 Sqn	Melbourne	22 a/c
	51 Sqn	Snaith	22 a/c
	76 Sqn	Linton-on-Ouse	17 a/c
	77 Sqn	Elvington	18 a/c
	78 Sqn	Linton-on-Ouse	18 a/c
	102 Sqn	Pocklington	18 a/c
	158 Sqn	Rufforth	23 a/c
No 6 Group RCAF	405 Sqn	Topcliffe	21 a/c
	408 Sqn	Leeming	18 a/c
	419 Sqn	Middleton St George	18 a/c
No 8 Group	35 Sqn	Graveley	24 a/c

Chapter 4

Coastal Halifaxes

Nearly eight million tons of British, Allied and neutral shipping was sunk by enemy action in 1942. For Britain it was looking bleak as Admiral Doenitz's U-Boats sent cargo after cargo to the black depths of the Atlantic. For the AOC-in-C Coastal Command, Air Chief Marshal Sir Philip Joubert de la Ferté KCB, CMG, DSO, who took up his post on June 14, 1941, the answer was the acquisition of long-range aircraft to bridge the Atlantic gap where the U-Boats could hunt virtually unmolested.

For the German crews, aircraft were the greatest danger when travelling on the surface. Unlike modern submarines which can stay submerged almost indefinitely, wartime 'boats were forced to surface at intervals to recharge their batteries and it was also more efficient and faster to travel on the surface. When an air attack was imminent, it took a good crew on average 25sec for the alarm to be given and a U-Boat to submerge and once below the waves it stood a fair chance of surviving.

To gain a modicum of surprise and get as close to the target as possible before being spotted, Coastal Command conducted trials on the best colour to paint and try and conceal its aircraft. It came up with white sides, fins and rudders, with all top surfaces in the standard temperate sea scheme of Dark Slate Grey and Extra Dark Sea Grey. This combined with new search radar, ASV Mk 1 through to ASV Mk 3 (a version of Bomber Command's H2S), the Leigh Light for night searches, and more powerful depth bombs, aided with information obtained by Ultra at Bletchley Park which broke the German naval Enigma code, saved Britain from the starvation Hitler had planned.

Following the loan of some Bomber Command Halifaxes, RAF Coastal Command took delivery of some converted examples to meet the long-range general reconnaissance requirement. GR.II Series 1a HR686 J2 was one of these and is armed with a Type A four-gun dorsal turret. Under the fuselage is a 10cm ASV Mk III search radar which could detect a convoy at 40 miles and a surfaced submarine at 12 miles. It was operated by No 502 Sqn, but failed to return from a sortie on October 3, 1944. (via Barry Charles Wheeler)

A request for help

In 1941, to help plug the gap between America and Europe, RAF Coastal Command received 20 Consolidated LB-30Bs, later named Liberators, together with some PBY Catalina flying-boats. Early the same year, the then AOC-in-C Coastal Command, ACM 'Ginger' Bowhill, put in a plea for some Halifax bombers, but the request was rejected. Instead, a batch of 150 more Catalinas was ordered.

In 1942, as the situation in the Atlantic continued to deteriorate, Prime Minister Churchill stepped in and ordered the new Bomber Command AOC, ACM Harris to assist Coastal Command with some additional aircraft. Very reluctantly, he agreed to transfer six Avro Lancasters to help with patrol duties; these stayed until October 1942.

It was Operation Torch, the invasion of French West Africa in late '42, and the vulnerability of the troop ships to U-Boat attack that finally forced Harris to relinquish 20 Halifax IIs for use by Coastal Command. In late October 1942, 15 aircraft representing the whole of No 405 Sqn, RCAF, and five from 158 Sqn transferred to Beaulieu, Hampshire, and within three days, the former bomber crews became maritime patrollers and began anti-submarine flights over the Bay of Biscay. For their new role, the aircraft were modified to carry six 250lb depth bombs, together with three standard 330gal long-range tanks in the bomb-bay. Later, an enlarged 600lb anti-submarine bomb entered service which had more explosive power and could be dropped from higher altitude.

The first success came on November 11 when P/O Colledge's crew found a U-Boat being refuelled by two surface vessels. The group was successfully bombed and machine-gunned with considerable damage inflicted. Operations continued until December when the No 158 Sqn detachment returned to Bomber Command, followed in March 1943 by 405 Sqn.

This No 518 Sqn Halifax Met Mk V Series 1a flew meteorological air reconnaissance flights from UK bases from January 1944. Cunliffe-Owen at Eastleigh converted Mk Vs for the specialised task of reporting on the weather on flights far out over the North Atlantic and Western Approaches. On the data collected often hung decisions which would effect Allied operations in Europe. (via Philip Jarrett)

Among armament trials tested at A&AEE in late 1942 was the fitting of four rocket projectiles under each inner wing of Halifax Mk II JD212. This was intended for anti-U-Boat operations with Coastal Command, but ground firing was found to damage the front fuselage and no air trials were flown. (via Philip Jarrett)

Coastal-owned and operated – at last

In March 1943, Coastal Command began operations with its own Halifaxes, specially converted from Rootes-built bombers by Cunliffe-Owen at Eastleigh, Hants. They had an all-up weight of 60,000lb and incorporated 690gal long-range tanks in the bomb-bay, ASV radar and a strengthened gun position in the nose for a 0.5in Browning to give some basic fire-power as the aircraft approached the target. It was proposed that the aircraft be fitted with air-to-ground rockets like those arming Coastal Beaufighters and Mosquitoes, but trial fitments of eight rocket rails on Mk II Srs IA JD212, four each side of the forward fuselage, so damaged the aircraft skin that the idea was abandoned.

The first Coastal squadron to receive the modified Merlin 20/22-powered Halifax GR.IIs was No 58 Sqn at the end of 1942, replacing its slow, ageing Whitleys and moving to Holmesley South in Hampshire in March. They were joined by No 502 Sqn and both were declared operational with their new aircraft flying from both Holmesley South and St Eval in Cornwall.

With the new 10cm ASV Mk III search radar fitted, together with Boozer, a radar aid which indicated whether the aircraft had been picked up by enemy search radar, Coastal Command appeared likely at last to gain a greater measure of success against the U-Boats.

Fighter versus Bomber

Attacking the U-Boats from the air was not easy and was made much more uncomfortable when the submarines stayed on the surface and poured AA fire from multiple-barrelled cannon from newly-fitted 'band-stand' extensions to the conning tower. This claimed a number of RAF aircraft – Wellingtons, Sunderlands and Halifaxes – while further danger came from four Staffels of twin-engined Junkers Ju 88C-6 fighters of V./KG 40 which had been transferred to Fliegerfuhrer Atlantik based at Bordeaux-Marignac on the west coast of France.

Intended to help protect the U-Boats as they transited between their French bases and the operational areas, the heavily armed fighters generally hunted in packs over the Bay and were bad news for the slower, older RAF aircraft. One encounter with these formidable machines took place in April 1943 when BB276, a 58 Sqn Halifax on a lone patrol, was spotted by a group of seven Ju 88s. Jettisoning its depth bombs, the 'white' hunter became the hunted as it fought a 47-minute battle with the enemy force. Twisting and turning, the big four-engined bomber proved frustratingly indestructible to the German pilots, the Halifax gunners inflicting damage on three of the Ju 88s with the remainder calling off the engagement. Much relieved, the RAF crew landed back at St Eval, Cornwall, with little to show for their battle, apart from one bullet hole in the tailplane and three dents in a turret fairing! In March, each squadron lost aircraft to enemy action. On the 22nd, Flg Off McCullock was on patrol in the Bay of Biscay when he spotted a U-Boat on the surface heading for port. This was U-338 which had been damaged in a previous attack. German Kapitanleutnant Manfred Kinzel elected to stay surfaced and fight which he did and shot down BB314 on its bombing approach. Only the flight engineer Sgt Taylor survived, being picked up by the submarine and made a PoW.

The second loss was on March 29 and involved Halifax HR688 of 502 Sqn, commanded by Plt Off Davey. Meeting an in-bound convoy, Davey began a protecting search looking for signs of the enemy. He found a surfaced U-Boat preparing to attack the rearmost ships and successfully depth-bombed the vessel. With the weather closing in, Davey left the convoy escorts to pick up any survivors and set course for base. However, he failed to break free of the cloud and after being airborne for 12 ¼ hr, ordered the crew to bale out. Fortunately, all landed safely, the aircraft crashing on Exmoor.

Through the summer and autumn months of 1943, both squadrons maintained patrols, attacking U-Boats, sometimes successfully, and other times less so. The Ju 88s too continued to meet the Halifaxes. Losses for 58 Sqn included BB277 flown by Flg Off Ayles on March 24, HR743 with the crew of Flt Sgt Hoather on May 9, BB257 with Flt Sgt Gilmore on June 1, and one each on August 15 and 16 when HR745 and HR746 commanded by Flt Sgt Dunbar and Flg Off Jenkins respectively, were shot down. Partly in response to such losses, Coastal Beaufighters began anti-Ju 88 patrols, turning the tables on the German crews who were used to easier game!

In October, night attacks were flown using radar to detect the submarines and flares to illuminate them for bombing and by early 1944, 58 Sqn were averaging 70 sorties a month with more surface vessels becoming targets. As the Normandy invasion neared, the squadrons incorporated the task of blocking off the Channel from U-Boat infiltration. More submarines were attacked, three by 502 Sqn in June 1944.

A U-Boat surrenders in May 1945, its black flag flying from the conning tower on which some of the crew view the passing aircraft. (via Barry Charles Wheeler)

As the Allies established a foothold in France and the Atlantic coast bases were cleared of the enemy, the two Halifax squadrons moved north to Stornoway in the Hebrides for more anti-submarine patrols up to Iceland and along the Norwegian coast. In December 1944, No 502 Sqn received more capable Hercules-engined Halifax IIIs and in April No 58 Sqn also took delivery of this version. With VE-Day, both squadrons were disbanded.

'The weather today…'

Weather forecasting was vital for both sides and much time and effort as well as losses was expended in acquiring data for the planning of air and sea operations. For example, the bombing campaign against Germany and from 1943 preparations for the Allied invasion of Europe relied heavily on the accuracy of weather information and such knowledge and the gathering of data became a matter of national secrecy.

Met reconnaissance flights around the UK coast began in 1940 and the following year were brought under the jurisdiction of Coastal Command. Initially using the aircraft's navigator to gather the information, it was subsequently realised that there was a need for trained meteorological observers and these personnel began arriving on the Met Flights in 1943. The flights were numbered in the 1400 series, but in 1943-44, six Flights were of sufficient size to be re-constituted as squadrons.

Halifaxes joined No 1404 Flight, Coastal Command, in December 1943. They were Mk Vs modified by Cunliffe-Owen and incorporated an additional station for the Meteorological Observer in the nose, deletion of the nose gun, an external probe known as a psychrometer to measure the outside air temperature and humidity, a special radio altimeter to calculate sea level pressures and extra fuel tanks to give the aircraft greater range. The navigation equipment was expanded to include Loran for long-range fixes, Gee, ASV and an American B3 drift meter.

In February 1944, No 1404 Flight became No 517(Met) Sqn, moving to Brawdy in Pembrokeshire, the force expanding with 518 Sqn at Tiree, 519 Sqn at Wick (later Leuchars), 520 Sqn at Gibraltar and 521 at Chivenor in Devon.

From their bases, the Met Halifaxes flew predetermined and precise routes known by code-names such as Bismuth, Mercer, Epicure, Recipe and Magnum, and flown twice in every 24hr, except the aircraft based at Tiree in the Western Isles which flew four times in every 24hr. Only in the most appalling weather were flights stopped, but where possible, operations were flown to gather the data. Despite losses, sometimes due to engine fires or bad weather, the regularity of these important sorties was maintained until the end of the war.

Gathering the information involved flying set patterns with positions on the 700nm track from base at 50nm intervals when the aircraft would fly a series of step climbs and descents recording pressure readings. From sea level to 20,000ft the aircraft took the recordings and transmitted the figures back to base every half-hour. The crews based in Tiree would on average fly operations every four days and every three months be given ten days leave.

Some of the Halifax GR.IIs and IIIs used by Coastal Command:
BB256, BB262, BB268, BB276, DT636, DT642, DT665, DT692, HP255, HR688, HR693, HR741, HR744, HR774, HR782, HR792, HR815, HR983, HX152, HX177, HX223, HX225, JB901, JD176, JD178, JD245, JP165, JP166, JP173, JP271, JP298, JP300, JP333, JP339. NA226, NA235, PN183, PN202, PN399, RG363, RG364, RG369, RG395.

Some of the Halifax IIIs, Vs and VIs used by Met squadrons:
V9123, DG288, DG304, DG316, DT642, HX344, LK682, LK688, LK692, LK704, LK706, LK966, LK997, LK998, LL144, LL145, LL186, LL216, LL220, LL221, LL295, LL296, LL393, LL485, LL517, MZ390, MZ462, NA165, NA223, NA231, NA247, PN190, RG385, RG390, RG780, RG787, RG843, ST798, ST809.

Chapter 5

Learning to Cope – The Halifax HCUs

Learning to handle the Halifax was a hurdle all pilots' posted to fly the type had to undergo. Early training on the aircraft was initially the task of the first squadrons equipped with B.Is, No 28 Conversion Flight forming in August 1941 within No 4 Group at Linton-on-Ouse. However, it was clear that as aircraft deliveries increased more units would be needed to process the increasing numbers of aircrew required.

Crew training was the task of the Heavy Conversion Units equipped with former front-line and often very battered aircraft which had survived operations and been replaced by new production examples. The instructors were mainly posted in from the bomber squadrons and taught the fledgling pilots all they could to prepare them for the rigours of fighting the war from a Halifax cockpit. (*Flight*)

Training accidents took a steady toll of aircraft and trainees, with undercarriage collapses, engine fires and loss of control being most widely recorded. Typical was this accident to Halifax II Series 1 (Special) W7927 of 1658 HCU, which crashed on landing at Fairwood Common on April 10, 1944, after suffering engine failure on a cross-country flight from its base at Riccall. (via Barry Charles Wheeler)

Early in 1942, the first Heavy Conversion Units (HCU) were formed, one per Group. The first was No 1652 HCU for No 4 Group at Marston Moor, which absorbed No 28 CU, followed by No 1658 at Ricall and 1659 at Leeming, both part of No 4 Group, but the latter moving to work with No 6 (RCAF) Group in January 1943. Others were formed later in 1942 and 1943. They were equipped mainly with early war-weary Halifax Is, IIs and Vs, withdrawn from the front line as newer aircraft arrived.

Flying the old war-horses was a trial in itself, for a Halifax in inexperienced hands was a perilous machine. It was difficult to taxi, it had an undercarriage-straining swing on take-off and demanded special care on landing. The aircraft the novices were to train on had been bashed around, heavy hands had fought the night war over Germany, and it showed as the fledgling pilots climbed into the cockpit. Trainee Bill Webb was a novice pilot when he arrived at No 1652 HCU and began a conversion course on the Halifax.

'All the aircraft had done several tours of operations and were really "clapped out". To fly a cross-country, it was necessary to start at one end of a long line of Halifaxes and try to find one that responded to the pre-flight checks and actually started. Few were fully serviceable, but if most of the systems worked, you considered it was worth taking and out we taxied.

'Among the many basic problems encountered during the course was the proneness for the Merlin-powered Halifax to engine failure. You were suddenly aware that the temperature on one of the engines was at nearly boiling point and this seemed to kick-off another one. You soon switched off the problem engine and feathered the prop and the skipper quickly called the distress frequency known as Darkie, to get clearance for a straight-in approach and landing.'

Other problems were leaking fuel tanks, weakened undercarriages from earlier squadron use, and the ever present fear of rudder overbalance where the rudders induced a large sideslip angle which was enough to stall or almost stall the fins on tight turns in the circuit where there was no height to correct the problem, a fatal situation which claimed the lives of many crews, both trainee and operational (later cured by adoption of the larger Type D fin). As well as training to handle the Halifax, crews learnt to drop bombs, 11lb flash practice bombs on designated ranges.

When Leonard Cheshire arrived at Marston Moor in 1942, he recognised the problems faced by new arrivals. He briefed them on all aspects of the training programme. Such as 'watch the flap and bomb-door handles – they are easily confused. And don't touch the handle over the pilot's seat – it's the cockpit hood release!'

It wasn't all conversion work at the HCUs, for senior pupils, tour-expired navigators and instructors were ordered to contribute to the Thousand Bomber Raids, first to Cologne in May 1942 with 12 aircraft of which 11 came back, followed the next night to Essen. On June 25, 1,067 aircraft attacked Bremen, but 48 were lost and 65 damaged with over three times as many aircrew killed as those who died on the ground.

Training with a Difference

Not all four-engine conversion took place at HCUs. For the gutsy ferry pilots of the Air Transport Auxiliary (ATA), such as the tall, athletic 25-year-old Lettice Curtis, the recommendation that she undertake a multi-engine course was seen as a lucky move. After all, she was the only woman in an all-male Ferry Pool, which was not always an easy association.

Awaiting its next training flight at Croft airfield in Yorkshire, Halifax B.V Series 1 (Special) EB199 was on the strength of No 1664 HCU before crashing at Atley Hill, South Cowton, Yorks, on October 22, 1943. (via Barry Charles Wheeler)

Post-war, crews were still being trained to fly the rapidly diminishing number of RAF Halifaxes still flying. This example, an A.VII NA421 was one of five with No 1385 Heavy Transport Support Conversion Unit which formed at Wethersfield in April 1946, only to disband three months later. (via Barry Charles Wheeler)

In 1942, the ATA acquired its own Halifax, BD191, for converting the ferry pilots on to large bombers which were beginning to leave the assembly factories for onward transfer to the squadrons. It had been built by the London Aircraft Production Group, the third of 200 B.IIs produced by the Leavesden factory, and would remain there for ATA use. It later served with No 1652 HCU before ending its life, as many did, with an undercarriage collapse at Marston Moor in January 1944.

As Lettice Curtis recounts, 'Leavesden consisted of one 1,000-yard runway, one end of which sloped down towards the hangars where the Halifax was kept. It was not a suitable place for practice circuits and landings and thus, whenever the aircraft was reported to be serviceable, the two of us that were on the course at the time would go over with our Polish instructor, Klemens Dlugaszewski, or Dluga as we called him, to Leavesden and he would fly the aircraft out to some airfield willing to have us that had a runway roughly into wind. We took it to Bovingdon and Bassingbourne and on one occasion to Hampstead Norris near Newbury.

'It was a foggy autumn. Between bad weather and the Halifax unserviceability, flying to say the least was spasmodic. We went to Bovingdon and I carried out four dual circuits. The aircraft was certainly a lump to handle but not all that more so than a Wellington; one could not afford to let either of them get out of trim. It was the ailerons that called for the nearest thing to brute strength on this aircraft and I often feel that the muscles in my shoulders owe more to the Halifax than to many years playing tennis.

'For the first time there was somebody else in the aircraft in the person of a flight engineer who could really help. He could retract the undercarriage and flaps, close the throttles finally on landing and ensure that they didn't slip back on take-off, leaving one free to hold the spectacle type grip on the control column with both hands during take-off and landing.

'On October 26, 1942, I was at White Waltham with other members of the ATA for a visit by Mrs Roosevelt who was studying the activities of women in wartime Britain. It was a pouring wet day and I was standing under the wing of a Halifax which had been brought to White Waltham for the occasion, when I was inevitably introduced as the first woman to be trained on four-engined bombers. Next day the papers, as they will, latched on to this and regardless of the fact that I hadn't even gone solo published headlines "Mrs Roosevelt meets Halifax Girl Pilot" and "Girl Flies Halifax".

'The next day I finally went solo which in this case consisted of Dluga getting out and leaving me and the flight engineer, Mr F Lees, to get on with it. It was not so much a moment of achievement as one of acute relief that at last, the first bridge at least had been crossed.' Lettice Curtis continued her course and went on to deliver 222 Halifax aircraft from the production factories to Bomber and Coastal Command squadrons.

ATA pilot, Lettice Curtis, climbs into a Spitfire, but she was equally skilled as a delivery pilot of brand-new Halifax bombers. (via Barry Charles Wheeler)

Chapter 6

Halifax – Nightly through Flak and Fighters...

In the freezing night air high over Germany, Luftwaffe ace Helmut Lent in his Messerschmitt Bf 110G twin-engine fighter stalked a Halifax bomber. Moving closer beneath the 'Tommy', still unseen but flying parallel to the bomber's line of flight, Lent finally positioned his fighter below and slightly behind the huge dark shape above. Knowing he couldn't miss this large target at such a close range, the German pressed the gun button and a stream of 20mm high explosive shells poured into the bomber, blasting along the port wing and engines before Lent moved his control column to the right to track the destruction into the fuselage. In seconds the wing erupted in flames as the fuel tanks ignited. Lent banked sharply away to find another victim as the fatally damaged Halifax turned over to begin its final descent to the ground.

Oberst Lent, who died in a landing accident in October 1944 with a score of 110 victories, had flown an attack typical of those conducted by Luftwaffe night-fighter pilots from the autumn of 1943 when the Luftwaffe employed its latest weapon against the RAF bombers. The Bf 110G had a modified armament

Abandoned in Norway at the end of the war, Messerschmitt Bf 110G-4 B4+KA was operated by 4./NJG 3 night-fighter unit and carries the 'built-in head-wind' aerial array of a FuG 220 SN-2 radar. Black was sprayed under the starboard wing and lower engine nacelle to identify the aircraft for friendly searchlights and flak units. (via Barry Charles Wheeler)

Ungainly and unloved, early twin-engine Dornier Do 217J versions of the E-2 bomber were known to night-fighter crews as 'tired crows' and were initially stop gap night-fighters in 1942 until sufficient Bf 110s became available. In the nose was a FuG 202 AI radar array. Both the 217J and the improved 217N (below,right) were later fitted with four 20mm MG 151 upward-firing cannon in a Schrage Musik installation, seen below in the top centre of the fuselage. (via Barry Charles Wheeler)

Oberst Helmut Lent, one of the Luftwaffe's high-scoring aces with 110 kills. (via Barry Charles Wheeler)

layout known as Schrage Musik or Jazz Music. This consisted of a pair of 20mm MG FF/M cannon mounted in the centre fuselage and arranged to fire upwards and forwards at an angle of between 10° and 20°. For sighting, the pilot used an extra reflector sight mounted above his head. Such was the withering hail of shells fired at relatively close range into the vulnerable underside of the wing and engines that the RAF crews never knew what hit them!

Instead of relying on the battery of nose-mounted guns to shoot down their quarry from behind and often dodging the fire from the rear gunner, the German night-fighters adopted this new style of interception to begin a period of remarkable success, bringing down scores of bombers. Many of the aircraft attacked simply exploded and returning crews were reporting these big fireballs, only to be told by station intelligence officers they were 'scarecrows' – fired into the sky by German AA gunners to unnerve the attacking force. The new armament layout remained a well-kept secret until, early in1944, several bombers survived such attacks and on examining the damage, the cause of the many unexplained losses was revealed.

As related elsewhere, some of the Halifax squadrons adopted the Preston-Green ventral turret mounting a 0.50in gun to scare off attacks from below.

Early German Defence

In the early raids on targets within Germany, the RAF did little damage with the fleets of twin-engine Bristol Blenheims, Handley Page Hampdens, Armstrong Whitworth Whitleys and Vickers Wellingtons. The night sorties had yet to become fully co-ordinated and the bombing was usually well outside the target area. While flak would sometimes be troublesome and occasionally claim victims among the slow-flying attackers, the biggest and most capricious enemy for the fledgling crews was the weather. Traditionally, winter over northern and central Europe was a period of low cloud, heavy icing conditions, strong winds and snow, which combined to throw effective flying operations into disarray.

For Germany, the biggest gap in its wide-ranging arsenal was the lack of home-based air defence. The strategic planners in Berlin had developed an all-embracing tactical air force, but with two missing elements – a long-range strategic bomber and a strong defensive force to protect the country's war industry. The former would never be achieved, while the latter was dismissed at a pre-war conference with – 'Night fighting! It will never come to that'! However, it did, but crucial development in the sphere of radar lagged behind that of the British, a factor which dogged German technicians as they desperately tried to make up for ground lost in the early years.

Nachtjagd 1942

Luftwaffe chief Hermann Goering ordered the formation of a night-fighter or Nachtjagd force in July 1940 and entrusted General Josef Kammhuber to set up the first night fighter Division. They deployed upwards of 150 day fighters – the Messerschmitt Bf 110E and F modified as night interceptors – and a fighter version of the Dornier Do 17Z. Later, two bomber types were developed for the night-fighting role, the Dornier Do 217J and Junkers Ju 88C. The Dornier proved a disappointment with a troublesome undercarriage, insufficient power and lacking manoeuvrability, but the more versatile Ju 88, steadily updated, remained with the force throughout the rest of the war.

Carrying RAF colours with a yellow P-Prototype marking on the fuselage, serial TP190 was the captured Ju 88G-1 4R+UR of 7./NJG 2 which landed at RAF Woodbridge in error on July 23, 1944. As well as the SN-2 radar, it was also fitted with FuG 227 Flensburg wing antennas and a four-cannon belly pod. (via Barry Charles Wheeler)

To equip the aircraft for their specialist role, Telefunken developed the FuG 202 Lichtenstein airborne radar with a range of two-and-a-half miles. During initial trials with the new system, Oblt Ludwig Becker flying a Dornier Do 215B achieved its first success on August 9, 1941, when he shot down a 309 Sqn Wellington over Hamburg. Production of the new radar was slow to start, but sets began arriving from the spring of 1942. On the ground, Freya and Giant Wurzburg radars able to see some 40 miles and forming a Himmelbett (Four-Poster Bed) system of reporting areas, gave sufficient warning of approaching enemy bombers to enable ground controllers to scramble and direct the fighters into position.

However, the first RAF Thousand Bomber raid mounted against Cologne on May 30, 1942, proved to the Germans that nothing could repel such a force even though a loss of 41 aircraft or 3.8% of the force was a notable effort by the flak and fighter crews.

Enter the 'Heavies'

Early in 1941, the four-engined Short Stirling and HP Halifax began appearing over Europe, followed in March 1942 by the Avro Lancaster. For the Germans, these were formidable machines, faster, protected by armour and gun turrets, with an overall performance greater than the smaller bombers they were replacing. Indeed, at height, a lightly loaded Halifax stood a good chance of outrunning a Bf 110!

By February 1942, the German night-fighter force had expanded to seven Gruppen with 367 aircraft, although unserviceability severely reduced the force by some 50%. The hoped-for more modern replacement – the Messerschmitt 210 – proved useless in the night role, so production of the Bf

110 which had ceased, was re-started in the autumn of 1941 with orders to deliver up to 42 aircraft a month. By the end of 1942, the Luftwaffe had a strength of five Geschwader with 15 Gruppen (a Gruppe comprised three or four Staffeln each with nine aircraft plus a staff unit with three), increasing within six months to six operational and a training Geschwader with a total of 22 Gruppen.

In the summer of 1942 trials of upward-firing guns which had been first proposed by an armourer, Paul Mahle, were flown at the experimental establishment at Tarnewitz. Encouraged by the results, field tests were flown in 1943, Oblt Schoenert scoring the first kill in a Bf 110 over Berlin in May. In the coming weeks, the oblique gun mounting was refined and installations began on operational aircraft. In the meantime, the RAF had begun marking targets with greater accuracy, thanks to the Path Finder Force, newly created by Bomber Command, and using a Master of Ceremonies to control the bomber streams.

The RAF was also getting the measure of the German radar systems. From September 1942, the Freya ground control radar was being jammed, while in the skies, Monica was introduced, the aerial located just below the rear turret to warn of the approach of enemy fighters – although determining whether the aircraft behind was friend of foe was still an insurmountable problem. Boozer was a device tuned to the frequencies of Wurzburg and Lichtenstein radars to warn a bomber that it had been picked up, but again, false alarms were frequent.

One stroke of good fortune to befall the British – and a crushing blow to the Germans – was the defection on May 9, 1943, by a night-fighter crew from Norwegian-based 10./NJG 3 flying a Ju 88R-1 equipped with FuG 212. It revealed that Wurzburg and Lichtenstein worked on the same frequency, thus requiring only one means of jamming to neutralise Luftwaffe air and ground radars. Thus,

Integral with Germany's night-fighter force was the ground-based Wurzburg radar. This detected the bomber streams as they approached the German border, but strips of metal foil known as Window could jam the frequency, blotting out returns used to plot the passage of the attackers. This former Dutch example was returned to its country of origin and is an exhibit at the Luftwaffe Museum at Berlin Gatow. (via Barry Charles Wheeler)

Two night-fighter foes together in the RAF Museum Hendon Battle of Britain Hall. In the foreground, the Bf 110G-4 which appeared at the 1945 Captured Aircraft Display at Farnborough, and behind, the Ju 88R-1 which defected from Norway on May 9, 1943. The latter gave the British full details on the working of the FuG 212 Lichtenstein air intercept radar and was pitted against a Halifax bomber to help neutralise the system. (via Barry Charles Wheeler)

the RAF began using thin strips of aluminium foil, known as Window, to jam the enemy systems. Uniquely, the Ju 88R-1 which played such an important part in reducing RAF bomber force losses can be seen today as an exhibit at the RAF Museum Hendon.

Uncontrolled Boars

As the raids increased in size during the autumn of 1943, the Luftwaffe desperately introduced other tactics against the bombers. One was the free ranging search and attack by single-seat Focke-Wulf Fw 190 and Bf 109 fighters, code-named Wilde Sau (Wild Boar). The idea of Major Hajo Hermann, the pilots of the first of three Geschwaders, JG 300, listened in to the Korps command post, but were not guided to the targets by the controllers. Gaining an indication where the attack was likely to take place, they took off and headed through the night sky. Often following illuminated lanes made by searchlights and star shells fired by flak guns to where the bombers could be found, the pilots began a 'free hunt' for targets and during the summer months operations proved surprisingly successful.

For example, in August 1943, the Wilde Sau units shot down 200 bombers of a total of 250 claimed by the night-fighter force. The downside was the loss of 61 twin-engine fighters with 40 pilots killed. However, the onset of the long winter nights saw lone pilots chasing bombers increasingly in poor weather with few opportunities to mount successful interceptions. Accidental losses mounted and it became a normal occurrence for as many as 25 aircraft of 60 that took off, to crash with not one success to show for it. The attrition suffered forced the Luftwaffe High Command to drop the free range flights in February 1944.

Another attempt to destroy the bombers was Zahme Sau or Tame Boar, developed by Oberst von Lossberg in which night-fighters would join the bomber stream and transmit direction-finding signals to attract other fighters. They would remain with the stream as it returned to England, attacking targets until their fuel ran low, before heading for a home base.

Battle of the Boffins

With the RAF now regularly using Window (the German equivalent was known as Duppel) to blank out the radars, German scientists devised an anti-jamming aid for the Wurzberg and modified the airborne Lichtenstein radar to change frequencies. Telefunken was still encountering problems with its next radar, the SN-2, mainly involving close-range definition on the screen and of 300 manufactured by early November 1943 only 12 of 49 delivered to the Luftwaffe were usable.

However, the German scientists overcame the problem and enhanced the system by deleting two of the original five screens which simplified the task of the operator and by May 1944, the 1,000th set had been delivered. Other successes were the Flensburg-Halbe which detected emissions from British tail-warning radars up to a distance of 62 miles (100km), and the FuG 350Z Naxos Z which picked up emissions from the H2S navigation radar up to a range of 31 miles (50km). It was hoped that these improvements in detection would help find and destroy the Pathfinders and the all-important Master of Ceremonies aircraft which were ensuring greater accuracy in laying waste to Germany's cities and its industry.

As the Halifax and Lancaster squadrons maintained their operations, often sustaining losses that swung between nil and upwards of a staggering 70 aircraft with the loss of some 500 men per night, the Germans had their own difficulties. The twin-engine de Havilland Mosquito was one problem which became deadly for the crews of the Nachtjagd. Aided by Serrate which homed on to radar emissions from the night-fighters, these agile interceptors hunted the Luftwaffe among the bomber streams. General Josef Schmid who replaced Kammhuber in November 1943 when the latter fell out with Goering, spoke highly of the 'wooden wonder' when interrogated after the war. He said that while material damage caused by the Mosquito raids was not decisive, their nuisance value was considerable. They forced the Germans to increase the numbers of air raid warnings by day and night and had a strong effect on production and on the nerves and morale of the population.

Special anti-Mosquito units tried to detect and destroy the fast, long-range twins, but victories were few as the Mosquitoes despatched some of the Nachtjagd's high-scoring aces and scooted around the German airfields, ground-staffing and often catching returning fighters, low on fuel, as they were landing after their battles with the bombers.

On October 23, during the raid on Kassel, the RAF employed a new tactic. As the bomber stream headed across Germany, the enemy controllers were trying to guess the target and they settled on Frankfurt. The British turned towards Kassel, but a German-speaking controller ordered the night-fighters to continue heading towards Frankfurt. Confusion reigned as counter orders were issued by the authentic command HQ, while the spoof controller sat back in Britain and countermanded the orders! It no doubt saved some of the raiders, but 42 bombers were shot down for the loss of six fighters.

With radio communications unreliable, the Germans devised a new code for the pilots by broadcasting music over their Forces radio station; dance music meant Berlin was the target, shanties Hamburg, carnival songs Cologne-Dusseldorf, pub songs Munich, etc. In response, the British played Hitler's speeches, bagpipes or just blotted out the radio station altogether by a continuous signal.

The Blitz on Berlin that ACM Harris had promised would raze the German capital to a flattened, defeated city, was going badly for the RAF. It had begun in November with British losses steadily

Still in good condition at Werneuchen, the German experimental airfield east of Berlin, are the wartime hangars where technicians worked long hours to install radar systems in the Luftwaffe night-fighters. The interiors too (below), exhibit little deterioration from when Bf 110s and Ju 88s were maintained within their well-built structures. (via Barry Charles Wheeler)

rising. Through January 1944, Halifax losses in particular were becoming untenable, so much so that Harris ordered the withdrawal of all Halifax B.IIs and Vs from Main Force operations – in a stroke, ten squadrons disappeared from the front line. In 14 raids on Berlin, the RAF lost 386 aircraft of which 70 were Halifaxes. But it was not all one-sided. On January 21, one of Germany's top-scoring night-fighter pilots, Maj Prince Sayn-Wittgenstein with 83 kills to his credit was shot down by a Mosquito, while Hptm Manfred Maurer, CO of I/NJG 1 died when his new Heinkel He 219 was accidentally rammed by a Bf 110 – his score stood at 65 aircraft.

Turning the Tide

The bomber war balance sheet for December to April 1944 showed a heavy loss for the RAF, 1,100 aircraft had been shot down with the death or captivity of over 7,000 trained aircrew. Replacement men and new bombers were arriving at the British airfields, but for the Germans, there were no such advantages. Experienced aircrew were being lost in combat, the aircraft factories were attacked to slow deliveries if not production, and airfields where the main night-fighters were dispersed were being bombed. In addition, the Allies were now increasingly targeting Hitler's oil supplies.

In the tit for tat electronics world of measure and countermeasure, the British gained another valuable lead on July 13, 1944. At 04.25hr, a twin-engine aircraft landed at Woodbridge airfield in Suffolk. When the bus arrived to pick up the crew, it was clear to the RAF personnel that the aircraft was a Ju 88 and they had a very frustrated Nachtjagd crew to take to the NAAFI! Uffz Mäckle was a pilot with 7./NJG 2 and with Obgfr Olze and Möckl had been on a sortie against minelaying Stirling bombers. Finding their compass out of action, the inexperienced crew had taken bearings on a radio beacon which they thought was in the east but was in fact in England. Having almost run out of fuel when approaching the coast, they put down on the broad Woodbridge runway. Their Ju 88G-1 gave Bomber Command countermeasures for the SN-2 airborne radar, as well as valuable information on the passive homing devices, Flensburg and Naxos.

Within days, the countermeasures were deployed. To jam the SN-2, a new longer concertina-shaped type of Window was being ejected from the bombers to the extent that by September, the SN-2 proved almost useless for air interception. *Naxos* detected the centimetric waves produced by the H2S, the response being that the bombers would only switch on the radar when nearing the target, while Flensburg alerted the British that this device homed on to Monica rear-warning radar. As of September 1944, Monica was no longer used.

Following the Normandy invasion on June 6, 1944, the attacks on night-fighter bases forced increased use of dispersed airfields, but paradoxically, in December, the force recorded its largest-ever strength at 1,319 aircraft of which 982 were operational. The New Year increased the difficulties that beset the fighter force as overwhelming numbers of bombers bludgeoned their way to target after target. Oil supplies began to dry up, experienced aircrew were being killed and their young replacements became fodder for the Allied gunners.

In the closing months of the war, Bomber Command continued its assault by night with the US 8th Air Force keeping up its missions in daylight. The Luftwaffe night-fighter force still tried to inflict damage to the British campaign, but RAF losses steadily diminished. Even the firestorms of Dresden for Operation Thunderclap on February 13/14, 1945, resulted in only six Lancasters lost. The battle was all but won, but Harris' effort to win the war by carpet-bombing the cities failed. The German people, like the British before them, had endured the devastating attacks and the survivors maintained their morale and support for the motherland. It was the overwhelming numbers of Allied aircraft pulverising the German fuel production and transportation that hastened the final collapse of the Third Reich.

Werneuchen – Germany's Radar Test Base

Between the eastern outskirts of Berlin and the Polish border lies the sizeable airfield of Werneuchen. Before the war it was a major training base, a role it continued to support after September 1939, but in April 1942 this airfield was also given the specialised task of an E-Stelle or Test Centre supporting the development of German radio and radar by the RLM Technical Office. The selection of Werneuchen for this role was taken for the relatively close proximity of the main companies involved in radar work such as Telefunken, Siemens and AEG, around the Berlin area.

Lufthansa was subcontracted to undertake the modifications and experimental work required on the aircraft and, like Farnborough in England, technicians were on hand to supervise the work on the main systems being prepared for service. Like other Luftwaffe experimental establishments such as Rechlin, which worked closely with the Werneuchen E-Stelle, and the two Baltic coast establishments, Tarnewitz and Travemunde, the work undertaken was designated Geheim! or Secret.

Here, in 1942, tests were conducted on the Lichtenstein radars, the Hohentwiel system for detecting ships, and the Freya ground-based radar. Later work involved the first IFF devices, the Berlin centimetric wavelength radar and the advanced Morgenstern system. British jamming operations were also replicated, and countermeasures devised. In 1944, Nachtjagdgruppe NJG 10 undertook the flight-testing of new systems. As Germany's fortunes waned and the Soviet armies inflicted increasing losses on the retreating Wehrmacht, the imminent arrival of Soviet troops forced the withdrawal of the E-Stelle to Stade in February 1945. Shortly afterwards the entire operation fell into British hands.

Post-war, the airfield was taken over by the Soviet Air Force and became a MiG base until the reunification of Germany in 1990. The airfield was abandoned and now exists in a state of gradual decay.

Chapter 7

Halifax Finale

The night raid on Leipzig on February 19/20, 1944, was the final straw for Bomber Command regarding the use of early version Halifaxes, and the B.II and V were permanently withdrawn from Main Force operations over Germany. What prompted the decision was the heavy toll of aircraft lost on this attack, 34 of 255 despatched, 13.3% and 14.9% of those which reached the enemy coast after 'early returns' had turned back. The Lancasters also fared badly from enemy flak and fighters that night – 44 of 561 sent out – but 78 missing machines meant yet another heavy loss of valuable and courageous men who would not return.

Handley Page and the A&AEE Boscombe Down worked hard to correct the design faults of the Halifax and while its poor reputation within the Command was never going to leave it, the Hercules-engined B.III proved to be the first version which finally gave the crews an aircraft capable of a performance close to that of the much-lauded Lancaster and in some cases, arguably better. From early 1944, the B.III began arriving in quantity with the squadrons of No 4 Group and the mixed Halifax/Lancaster No 6 (Canadian) Group.

With first deliveries of the new Halifax B.III to No 466 (Australian) Sqn in October 1943, the RAF at last gained the bomber it had put its faith in back in 1941. Hercules radial engines gave the aircraft the performance long required, enabling it to carry a worthwhile bomb load at the same height and speed as the Lancaster. It sported the new fin shape which finally cured the rudder stall and with the added advantage of the now widely used H2S radar, the RAF ensured that most targets attacked would be hit with an accuracy long sought. At Boscombe Down, the first production B.III HX226, seen here, was trialled over 150hr in five weeks with serviceability good. (via Barry Charles Wheeler)

To improve defensive protection, the tail turret was changed on B.III HX238 to twin 0.5in guns with AGLT or Advanced Gun Laying (Turret) radar. Known to Bomber Command as 'Village Inn', it was automatically sighted, but with its limited use up to the German surrender, its performance was difficult to judge. (via Barry Charles Wheeler)

The last mark of Halifax to see service with Bomber Command was the B.VI, the prototype of which, LV838 is seen at Boscombe in early 1944. It had the extended wings of the later B.IIIs and geared rudder tabs to alleviate the type's tendency to swing if an engine failed on take-off, while being optimised for hot-and-high operations with Tiger Force in the Far East. A few of the 473 B.VIs built saw service, principally with the two Free French squadrons, No 346 and 347, and No 158 Sqn, from April 1945. (via Barry Charles Wheeler)

RAF Bomber Command flew hundreds of sorties, many in daylight, in support of the Allied armies as the Germans retreated eastwards. Calais was the target on September 24, 1944, but cloud hampered results, so the bombers returned the next day and are seen encountering similar conditions. Of the 872 that took part, 397 were Halifaxes of which three are visible in this picture. (via Philip Jarrett)

As winter turned to spring, the RAF switched much of its effort from targets in Germany to attacks against the enemy in France. This was designed to soften up areas prior to the D-Day invasion, and by the summer, No 6 (Canadian) Group alone could provide nearly 300 Halifax aircraft for one night's operation.

Through April and May, Bomber Command hit railway marshalling yards, weapon storage sites, airfields, coastal batteries and ports, across a swathe of Northern France to reduce large-scale enemy troop and armour reinforcements which were expected to occur after the impending June 6 invasion. On the night of June 5/6 itself, 1,012 bombers (including 412 Halifaxes) dropped over 5,000 tons of high explosive on Normandy coastal batteries and continued attacks on the enemy rear areas for the next two weeks.

Six days after D-Day, the Germans began their V-l flying bomb campaign against London. Although it was known that an attack was due, it was more a case of when and how deadly it would be. Bomber Command retaliated on the night of June 16/17, when Oboe-equipped Mosquitoes marked four sites on the Pas de Calais for 149 Halifaxes and 236 Lancasters. All bombed successfully and no aircraft were lost.

Harris at last agreed to prioritise oil as a main strategic target alongside the war industry and the cities for Bomber Command, adding to the heavy daylight raids by the US 8th Air Force which between them steadily reduced enemy stocks of the vital liquids which had kept the Third Reich war machine going for so long. In fact, on August 27, 1944, RAF heavies took a rare daylight trip to Homberg in Germany, the 216 Halifaxes and 13 Lancasters being aggressively protected by nine squadrons of Spitfires outbound and seven squadrons on the way back. There were no losses, but the Rhein-preussen synthetic oil refinery was hit.

Petrol for the Tanks

As the Allied armies fought their way eastwards and into the Low Countries, the supply of fuel by road from the Normandy beachhead was becoming seriously stretched and the mechanised elements forming the Allied spearheads were beginning to use up fuel quicker than the tankers could supply it.

With stocks dropping towards the point where the offensive appeared likely to grind to a halt, the RAF was called upon to air deliver jerricans of petrol from England to Melsbroek airfield in Belgium. Seventy Halifaxes of No 4 Group began fuel supply flights on September 25, flying 435 sorties during an eight-day period. Each aircraft carried around 165 jerricans which equated to approximately 750 gallons and the total amount flown over to the continent reached 325,000 gallons.

The Halifax B.VI entered the fray in small numbers early in 1945. This was similar to the B.III but had 1,675hp Bristol Hercules 100 radials in modified cowlings with a revised fuel system. It also incorporated the extended wing, crew heating, Series 1A nose and rectangular fins and rudders. The first aircraft flew on December 19, 1943, and the first production example, of 457 built by HP and EE, made its flight ten months later on October 10, 1944. The slow supply of engines didn't help deliveries and the version made little difference to the performance of the Halifax force during the closing months of the war.

Gisela Halts Complacency

As the Luftwaffe night-fighter force became increasingly stretched and the RAF Mosquito hunters made life more difficult for the hard-pressed German crews, the bombers took fewer losses and could at last see an end to the carnage as the noose tightened round the shrinking Reich. However, one last major operation was mounted by the enemy to remind everyone that the war was not yet won – *Unternehmen Gisela*.

On the night of March 3/4, 1945, the Luftwaffe sent around 100 Junkers Ju 88G-6 night-fighters of NJG 2, 3, 4 and 5 in three waves to follow the bombers as they returned from raids on the synthetic oil plant at Kamen and the Ladbergen aqueduct on the Dortmund-Ems Canal. More than 450 aircraft were preparing to land back at their bases when the German fighters struck. At least 20 bombers were shot down – 13 Halifaxes from 4 and 6 Group, five Lancasters, a Fortress and a Mosquito. Three Ju 88s crashed through flying too low and the last of these, an aircraft of 12./NJG 3 that came down near Elvington, was to be the final enemy aircraft to crash on English soil. With eight Lancasters missing from operations over Germany that night, the 28 aircraft loss brought the casualty rate to 3.6% of those despatched.

Two views of Halifax HR926, TL-L of 35 Sqn flown by the legendary Sqn Ldr Alec Cranswick, DSO, DFC. The squadron was part of the Pathfinder force, the only one with Halifaxes, and Cranswick was a particularly gifted pilot who achieved much during his short career. His loss on his 104th sortie – he is thought to have completed more than 130 operations – on July 4/5, 1944, was keenly felt in Bomber Command and particularly by Pathfinder boss, AVM Don Bennett. (via Barry Charles Wheeler)

For the German crews, the success was a pyrrhic victory. Post-war research indicated that at least 25 Ju 88s crashed or were lost without trace returning to their bases. The Luftwaffe claimed just 14 RAF aircraft, indicating that those lost probably accounted for the difference in the final total. A follow-up Gisela attack was attempted on the night of March 17, but the 18 German crews could only record one success, a solitary Lancaster of 550 Sqn on a training flight, shot down by Fw Hommel of III/NJG 2.

Last Ops

The controversial destruction of Dresden took place on February 13/14, followed by a major raid on Chemnitz on March 5. Of the 760 bombers which took part, 40 losses were attributed to the attack, although icing conditions accounted for nine aircraft from 6 Group, taking the total of Halifaxes lost to 25, including the first B.VI, RG502 of 102 Sqn at Pocklington which crashed near Volyne in Czechoslovakia.

Six days later, on March 11, the Command assembled the largest number of bombers for a single raid to date when 1,079 (293 Halifaxes) from all the groups attacked Essen. Only three Lancasters were lost, and the raid virtually completed the destruction of this Ruhr town. The following day, the previous record was broken when 1,108 aircraft (292 Halifaxes) flew to Dortmund and disgorged 4,851 tons on the already suffering city.

Bomber Command continued its attacks through the final two months of the war, giving support for the ground forces and stopping the enemy from mounting large-scale counterattacks. But even with a vastly reduced fighter defence, the RAF still succumbed to losses. During an attack by 308 Halifaxes and 158 Lancasters of 4, 6 and 8 Groups on the Frisian island of Wangerooge, six of the seven aircraft lost were the result of mid-air collisions of which five were Halifaxes from 76, 408 and 426 Sqn. And it was a further accident which claimed the last two aircraft of Bomber Command lost in the war, when two Halifax IIIs of 199 Sqn on a Mandrel screening mission in support of bomber operations over Kiel collided, causing the deaths of 13 aircrew.

It was Halifax III NA259 of 199 Sqn which has the dubious distinction of being the last of its type to be lost in Bomber Command service when it crashed at Cromer on air test on June 25, 1945.

All that was left of a Halifax, shot down by flak over Germany and one of thousands of aircraft lost on operations by RAF Bomber Command. (via Barry Charles Wheeler)

Halifax Squadrons, RAF Bomber COMMAND April 19, 1945			
No 4 Group	10 Sqn	Melbourne	30 a/c
	51 Sqn	Leconfield	32 a/c
	466 RAAF Sqn	Driffield	23 a/c
	76 Sqn	Holme	29 a/c
	77 Sqn	Full Sutton	25 a/c
	78 Sqn	Breighton	45 a/c
	102 Sqn	Pocklington	22 a/c
	158 Sqn	Lissett	41 a/c
	640 Sqn	Leconfield	25 a/c
	346 FAF Sqn	Elvington	31 a/c
	347 FAF Sqn	Elvington	33 a/c
No 6 Group RCAF	415 Sqn	East Moor	21 a/c
	425 Sqn	Tholthorpe	19 a/c
	408 Sqn	Linton	20 a/c
	420 Sqn	Tholthorpe	19 a/c
	426 Sqn	Linton	20 a/c
	427 Sqn	Leeming	1 a/c
	429 Sqn	Leeming	3 a/c
	432 Sqn	East Moor	22 a/c
	433 Sqn	Skipton-on-Swale	1 a/c
No 100 Group	171 Sqn	North Creake	20 a/c
	192 Sqn	Foulsham	18 a/c
	199 Sqn	North Creake	19 a/c
	462 Sqn	Foulsham	23 a/c

Note:

This order of battle reflects the on-going re-equipment of three squadrons within No 6 Group (No 427, 429 and 433) from Halifaxes to Lancasters. Training units equipped with the Halifax are not included.

Halifaxes in the Far East

While the European war drew to a bloody end, the Japanese were still fighting in the Pacific and the Far East, but for the Halifax, its role in those far-off theatres was minimal. Its presence there goes back to a series of trials undertaken by No 1577 Flight which took two aircraft, B.Vs DK254 and DK263, and two Lancaster B.IIIs JA903 and 904, out to India in October 1943.

Initial trials showed that the Halifaxes performed well in the hot climate, DK263 taking off in only 1,200yds on a Met flight from Calcutta in the blistering midday temperature at a max weight of 62,000lb, reaching 20,000ft in just over an hour. However, spares for all four aircraft were lamentably short, fortuitously, given the conditions, the first accident did not occur until some 800hrs of flying had been done, with DK254 suffering an undercarriage collapse following a cross-wind landing.

Gladbeck, on the northern edge of the Ruhr and on the line of advance for the Allied armies, was heavily bombed by No 6 and 8 Groups on March 24, 1945. Of the 175 aircraft that took part, 153 were Halifaxes and the sole casualty was MZ759 of No 158 Sqn from Lissett. Hit by flak, the aircraft is seen crashing in flames, only three of the crew managing to bale out to become PoWs. The Halifax, named *Wizard of Aus*, had completed a commendable 72 sorties since delivery in June 1944. (via Philip Jarrett)

A more serious landing accident occurred in January 1944, when DK263 flipped over at the end of a landing run killing nine of the 14 on board. It was November before two replacement Mk IIIs (NA642 and NA644) were ferried out to undertake towing trials with six gliders, four Horsas and two Hamilcars. Despite the often inhospitable climate, the various tugging combinations proved quite successful.

In May 1945, a second Halifax unit arrived in India to investigate enemy radar transmissions, No 1341 Flight bringing five aircraft for the task. While little new was discovered, the aircraft brought a useful transport capability for Air Command South-East Asia. With the end of the war, the Flight was charged with flying ex-POWs to Allied bases from where they could be transported home by sea.

Gliders Against the Japanese

Following the success of the towing trials, No 38 Group prepared to begin glider operations against the Japanese and a batch of 17 tropicalised Halifax Mk VIIs of 298 Sqn arrived in India in July 1945. The aircraft were fitted with large ventral freight panniers and during August they shuttled between India and Ceylon carrying weaponry, medicines and members of the 44th Airborne Division as they prepared for a battle that would never come. Halifaxes also flew the 'Hump' transport run into China from Calcutta (Dum Dum) to Kunming, and other flights to Singapore. One of the aircraft was stripped of its bombing paraphernalia and given seats for 24 passengers.

In March 1946, 298 Sqn was involved in Operation *Hunger*, famine relief for Burmese hill tribes that had stayed loyal to Britain through the war but were now threatened with starvation. By the end of the month, these former battlewagons had completed 80 sorties flying 887,415lb of rice to the affected areas. A further 81 sorties followed in April and after completion, the aircraft returned to their military support and heavy equipment dropping role. With spares still in short supply and flyable aircraft in increasingly reduced numbers, the squadron ended its days at Risalpur and in December 1946, disbanded and the aircraft struck off charge prior to scrapping.

Services in the Post-War World

When the war ended in Europe, almost overnight the Halifax was declared obsolete and withdrawn from main force bomber squadrons. Aircraft were ferried by their crews or by volunteer pilots wanting to make their last flight in the type, to collection airfields where they sat unwanted until contractors began to dismantle them in January 1946. From the airframe, only the engines were detached and

The crew of *Lili Marlene*, of No 158 Sqn at Lissett, gather by the tail turret to celebrate the shooting down of an enemy fighter and the artwork applied the next day by a proud ground crew. The aircraft, MZ366, would be lost on January 6, 1945, when it returned to base from a raid on Hanau and the pilot, Flt Sgt Anderson, RAAF, attempted a three-engine overshoot, crashing at North Frodingham. One died and all suffered injury. (via Barry Charles Wheeler)

stored. For No 4 and 6 Group squadrons, Rawcliffe or No 29 Maintenance Unit, High Ercall, was the final resting place for this bomber, unloved by the Air Staff from Harris down, but nurtured and respected by the crews that had flown it.

But not all Halifaxes disappeared. Those in No 38 Group repatriated POWs from Europe, alongside hundreds of Lancasters assigned the task. No 21 Heavy Glider Conversion Unit at Elsham Wolds began training in February 1945 and had an establishment of 12 Halifax Mk IIIs, plus Horsas. Improved Mk VIIs soon followed, all brand new, and trials continued with the unit moving to North Luffenham in December 1946, but it was to last for only 12 more months before it too was closed.

Superstition was widely felt throughout Bomber Command, but no jinx surrounded the most famous Halifax of all, *Friday the 13th*. It survived to complete 128 operations with Lissett-based 158 Sqn. A Handley Page-built B.III, LV907 was delivered on March 13, 1944 – hence the name – and 'F-Freddy' carried its crews safely through to its withdrawal from service on May 18, 1945. The first Halifax to achieve 100 missions (seen in the close-up view), it notched up a well-earned DSO, DFM and DFC for its crews. Flg Off Smith is seen with his men on completion of their tour with a score of 44 sorties marked on the nose. Finally, in June 1945 the aircraft was displayed on the site of John Lewis' bombed out store in Oxford Street with its total clearly displayed for all Londoners to see. It was subsequently dismantled and broken up for scrap. (via Barry Charles Wheeler)

'How many bomb aimers does it take…' in this case 39 when assembled for a group photograph in May 1945. The location was 102 Sqn at Pocklington. (via Barry Charles Wheeler)

Much work with the Army was the lot of some of the surviving Halifaxes. Typical was the role of the Airborne Transport Development Centre (AATDC) at Brize Norton which in July 1946 experimented with drops of the Short Term Supply Container from PP217. Other work involved drops of guns and jeeps and more Horsa tows using A.IXs RT814 and RT816.

Flying Training Command also held on to the Halifax. At Shawbury, the Empire Air Navigation School retained B.IIIs such as NA243, '276 and '279 alongside five modified B.VIs (PN188, '203, '206, '207 and RG352). No 1 Radio School at Cranwell had three B.VIs (RG874, '875 and '876), and the Empire Radio School at Debden operated its well-known B.VI RG815 *Mercury* which, in May 1946, flew a demonstration tour of overseas air forces including those of Iraq, India, New Zealand and Australia.

Above left and above right: Closer to the Reich's seat of power, the bombing of Berlin destroyed most of Hitler's government buildings. Above, is Herr Ribbentrop's Foreign Ministry in Wilhelmstrasse photographed in August 1945. Remarkably, further down the street, right, is Goering's treasured Air Ministry, the Reichluftfahrtministerium (RLM), which survived the swathe of destruction and is today Germany's Federal Finance Ministry. (US Army/Barry Charles Wheeler)

Coastal Command too retained Halifaxes, both for maritime patrol where it supplemented the Lancaster MR force, and keeping them with the long-range meteorological units. Now no longer hunting German U-Boats, No 518 Sqn flew Mk IIIs from March 1945 until GR.VIs replaced them a year later and in October the squadron was renumbered 202 Sqn but retained the aircraft until May 1951. The last Halifax flight with the Command was flown on March 17, 1952, when RG841 of 224 Sqn flew a final sortie from Gibraltar.

Right: 'Cook's tours' were laid on for ground crews and support staff after May 1945 to see the effect of the bombing offensive. This view shows the devastation wreaked on the Ruhr, although the exact location is not recorded. (via Barry Charles Wheeler)

Below: Another retiree was NA222, a Rootes Securities B.III previously with late-forming 640 Sqn at Leconfield, parked at High Ercall in February 1946. Outlined codes C8-O, glossy black sides and undersurfaces, and black and yellow check fin markings are typical of the colours applied to RAF bombers in the last months of the war. (via Barry Charles Wheeler)

Tropicalised A.Mk VII NA356 was one of a small number that helped increase transport capacity around the time of Japan's surrender. It is seen at Santa Cruz, India, in 1946 and carries an 8,000lb capacity ventral pannier. (via Barry Charles Wheeler)

Above and left: While most Halifaxes were withdrawn with seemingly undue haste immediately after the end of hostilities, a few remained in RAF use including RG815. This was a specially modified Mk VI of the Empire Radio School designed to demonstrate the latest in current radio equipment. In September 1946, appropriately named *Mercury*, it departed its base at RAF Debden and undertook a 29,000-mile flight to Australia, New Zealand and India, arriving back in the UK on November 21. The 12-man crew is seen with the Commandant of the ERS, Air Cdr Fagan on their return. (via Barry Charles Wheeler)

Top, middle and right: After surviving the air war over Germany, *Waltzing Matilda* had one last task to fulfil – a flight to Australia with some excited emigrants! Former wartime ATA pilot Captain GN Wickner purchased ex-466 Sqn Halifax B.III NR169 in November 1945 and with his wife and two children and 14 other people left Hurn in the converted G-AGXA on May 24, 1946. With seating for 15 passengers, plus baggage, the aircraft completed the trip to Sydney, Australia, in 71 flying hours, touching down at Mascot Airport on June 15. It was subsequently purchased by Air Carriers Ltd and re-registered VH-BDT but made only one flight before being grounded and eventually vandalised and scrapped. (via Aeroplane)

Chapter 8

'For Valour' – the Halifax VCs

Just one Victoria Cross was awarded to a crew member of a Halifax aircraft, Pilot Officer Joe Barton. A further VC was awarded to Wg Cdr Leonard Cheshire who had initially commanded Halifax squadrons but was not Gazetted solely for that. His award was for his unique contribution to operations with Bomber Command. Extracts from his Gazette entry are included below.

Cyril Joe Barton

Extract from *The London Gazette* of June 27, 1944

Pilot Officer Cyril Joe Barton (168669) RAFVR, No 578 Squadron (Deceased).

On the night of 30th March, 1944, Pilot Officer Barton was captain and pilot of a Halifax aircraft [B.III *Excalibur* LK797 based at Burn] detailed to attack Nuremberg. When some 70 miles short of the target, the aircraft was attacked by a Junkers Ju 88. The first burst of fire from the enemy made the intercommunication system useless. One engine was damaged when a Messerschmitt 210 joined in the fight. The bomber's machine guns were out of action and the gunners were unable to return fire.

Fighters continued to attack the aircraft as it approached the target area and, in the confusion caused by the failure of the communications system at the height of the battle, a signal was misinterpreted and the navigator, air bomber and wireless operator left the aircraft by parachute.

Pilot Officer Barton faced a situation of dire peril. His aircraft was damaged, his navigational team had gone and he could not communicate with the remainder of the crew. If he continued his mission, he would be at

Above left and above right: A smiling Plt Off Joe Barton stands in the centre of his crew before his courageous flight and posthumous award of the Victoria Cross. Left to right, wireless operator Sgt J Kay, bomb aimer Flg Off Crate, Barton, navigator Sgt L Lambert, and flight engineer Sgt M Trousdale. Kneeling in front, rear gunner Sgt F Brice and mid-upper gunner Sgt H Wood. On the right, Gp Capt Leonard Cheshire VC, OM.

the mercy of hostile fighters when silhouetted against the fires in the target area, and if he survived he would have to make a 4½ - hour journey home on three engines across heavily-defended territory. Determined to press home his attack at all costs, he flew on and, reaching the target, released the bombs himself.

As Pilot Officer Barton turned for home the propeller of the damaged engine, which was vibrating badly, flew off. It was also discovered that two of the petrol tanks had suffered damage and were leaking. Pilot Officer Barton held to his course and, without navigational aids and in spite of strong head winds, successfully avoided the most dangerous defence areas on his route. Eventually he crossed the English coast only 90 miles north of his base [Burn, Yorks].

By this time the petrol supply was nearly exhausted. Before a suitable landing place could be found, the port engine stopped. The aircraft was now too low to be abandoned successfully. Pilot Officer Barton therefore ordered the three remaining members of his crew to take up their crash stations. Then, with only one engine working, he made a gallant attempt to land clear of the houses over which he was flying. The aircraft finally crashed [at Ryhope Colliery, near Sunderland] and Pilot Officer Barton lost his life, but his three comrades survived.

Pilot Officer Barton had previously taken part in four attacks on Berlin and 14 other operational missions. On one of these, two members of his crew were wounded during a determined effort to locate the target despite the appalling weather conditions. In gallantly completing his last mission in the face of almost impossible odds, this officer displayed unsurpassed courage and devotion to duty.

Geoffrey Leonard Cheshire
Extracts from *The London Gazette* of September 8, 1944

Wing Commander Geoffrey Leonard Cheshire, DSO, DFC, RAFVR, No 617 Sqn
This officer began his operational career in June 1940. Against strongly-defended targets, he soon displayed the courage and determination of an exceptional leader. He was always ready to accept extra risks to ensure success. Defying the formidable Ruhr defences, he frequently released his bombs from below 20,000ft. Over Cologne in November 1940 [he was flying Whitley V P5005 of 102 Sqn from Linton-on-Ouse], a shell burst inside his aircraft, blowing out one side and starting a fire; undeterred, he went on to bomb the target.

At the end of his first tour of operational duty in January 1941, he immediately volunteered for a second. Again, he pressed home his attacks with the utmost gallantry. Berlin, Bremen, Cologne, Duisburg, Essen and Kiel were among the heavily-defended targets which he attacked [flying with the first Halifax squadron, No 35 at Linton]. When he was posted for instructional duties in January 1942 he undertook four more operational missions.

He started his third tour in August 1942 when he was given command of a squadron [No 76 at Middleton St George]. He led the squadron with outstanding skill on a number of missions before being appointed in March 1943 as a station commander [to Marston Moor as Group Captain].

In October 1943 he undertook a fourth operational tour, relinquishing the rank of Group Captain at his own request so that he could again take part in operations. He immediately set to work [as CO of 617 Sqn flying Lancasters] as the pioneer of a new method of marking enemy targets involving very low flying.

During his fourth tour which ended in July 1944, Wing Commander Cheshire led his squadron personally on every occasion. [He] has now completed a total of 100 missions [and would undertake three more to take his total to 103]. In four years of fighting against the bitterest opposition he has maintained a record of outstanding personal achievement, placing himself invariably in the forefront of the battle.'

Leonard Cheshire continued his extraordinary career, both within the Service where he witnessed the dropping of the atomic bomb on Nagasaki in 1945, to his post-war Christian life when he set up the Cheshire Foundation Homes for the Sick. He died on July 31, 1992, aged 74.

Chapter 9

'Setting Europe Ablaze'

The undercover world of spies, saboteurs and assassins in the Second World War is the story of brave men and women who fought behind the lines against the invader, both in Europe as well as overseas in countries occupied by the Axis Powers. Aircraft was the transport of choice to supply the secret armies with people and equipment, the two main operators of these being the Special Operations Executive (SOE) and the Secret Intelligence Service (SIS) – more widely known as MI6.

The first RAF unit assigned to secret work was No 419 Flight, formed in August 1940 at RAF North Weald with an establishment of four Westland Lysanders. Some Armstrong Whitworth Whitleys were soon acquired for longer flights and in March 1941, No 419 Flight was renumbered 1419 Flight before becoming No 138 Sqn in August under the command of Wg Cdr EV Knowles DFC. The seven Whitleys formed A Flight and the four Lysanders operated as B Flight. However, what was needed was a larger capacity aircraft for deeper penetration flights to supply the secret armies in Poland and Czechoslovakia.

With four engines and a handsome load-carrying ability, the Halifax was selected for the squadron and in October, the first Polish crew of Flg Off Jasinski and Sgt Sobkowiak (pilot and co-pilot), Flg Off Krol (navigator), and Sgts Soltysiak (flt engineer), Wasilewski (wireless op), Mol (rear gunner) and Chodyra (dispatcher), arrived at Linton-on-Ouse for conversion training on the bomber.

On November 7, 1941, they took Mk II L9612 on its first and what would turn out to be its last special operations sortie. Three personnel and six containers were dropped east of Poznan, but the Halifax

Undergoing maintenance at Brindisi, Italy, a 148 Special Duties Halifax B.V JP246 is prepared for another mission in July 1944. The following month, this and other aircraft would be closely involved with supplying the Polish Underground Army during the Warsaw Uprising. (via Barry Charles Wheeler)

The hazards of flying Special Duty operations for the SOE were highlighted on September 19/20, 1943, when Halifax Mk V DG252 of No 138 Sqn based at Tempsford was hit by flak and so badly damaged that the pilot, Flt Lt Dick Wilkins DFC ditched the aircraft off Harlingen, Holland, after dropping its cargo of arms and agents on the DZ. All five men aboard died. A second SD Halifax, BB317, also ditched in the North Sea that night, four of the seven crew surviving as PoWs. (via Barry Charles Wheeler)

experienced severe icing resulting in the hydraulic system failing and the main undercarriage coming down from its retracted position. The resultant drag meant a slow return flight – at 75mph ground speed – and not enough fuel to cross the North Sea. The crew elected to divert to neutral Sweden and made a successful forced landing at Tomelilla. They set fire to the aircraft and were briefly interned by the Swedes before flying back to the UK in a BOAC Hudson and returning to the squadron.

Two more Halifaxes arrived late in November, including Mk II, L9613, and it was in this aircraft that Flg Off P Hockey made a sortie to Czechoslovakia on December 28/29. His task was to drop six agents in three groups, two of which were communications and training squads, while the third was code-named 'Anthropoid' comprising Czech NCOs Kubis and Gabchik, assigned specifically to assassinate Reinhard Heydrich, the brutal SS *Reichsprotektor* of Bohemia and Moravia. They achieved their task on May 27, 1942, but at the cost of themselves, the savage destruction of the small village of Lidice and the murder of all its inhabitants.

Tempsford and a higher tempo

After a period operating from Newmarket and Stradishall, No 138 Sqn moved to Tempsford on March 14, 1942. As operations increased, Bomber Command chief, ACM Harris, who was somewhat less supportive of the special squadrons that had taken away some of his sought-after aircraft, felt they should be brought under his jurisdiction The Air Ministry rebuffed his proposal and decided 138 Sqn would be a separate entity, answering to the needs of SOE and SIS.

While the Lysanders hugged the south coast airfields, in particular Tangmere, to deposit and pick-up the 'Joes' across the Channel, the five Halifaxes on establishment took supplies and men to the underground networks, not only in Poland and Czechoslovakia, but also to France, Belgium, Holland, Denmark, and Norway.

A second special duties squadron, No 161, was established at Newmarket under Wg Cdr 'Mouse' Fielden MVO, AFC, in February 1942 from a nucleus supplied by the King's Flight. It moved first to Graveley before arriving with 138 Sqn at Tempsford in August 1942. Joining a varied collection of aircraft, the first of five Halifaxes arrived in September to replace Whitleys. To increase their range, the big aircraft were stripped of much of their interior equipment, the agents and crews thereafter experiencing a very basic form of travel with cold, draughty and spartan interiors; armament was limited to the four guns in the rear turret.

As Halifax Vs they could carry up to 15 standard 6ft-long C Type air-drop containers, three in each wing cell and nine in the main bomb bay. The H Type container comprised five separate cylindrical cells held together during the drop by a pair of metal rods. These were designed to be more easily broken down for concealment by reception committees on the ground.

For the dispatchers in charge of piles of softer parcels carried in the dark recesses of the rear fuselage, speed and efficiency were paramount when the drop-zone (DZ) was reached. Often assisted by another member of the crew, the dispatcher opened the two half-shell doors covering the circular hatch, locking them in place, and when given a 'green light', immediately pushed the parcels out into the slipstream. While the metal containers in the bomb bays usually contained weapons, grenades and ammunition, the softer parcels included everything else requested by the agents below. Speed was of the essence and an experienced dispatcher could push out half a ton in a matter of seconds. This reduced the time over the target as lingering was not recommended!

Air drops of containers were usually made at 500ft, once the pilot was satisfied the correct signal had been made, or 800ft if agents were to parachute in. For two-way voice communication between the aircraft and the agents on the ground, the aircraft were equipped with a VHF transmitter/receiver which had been developed by SOE. From an average of 13 drops a month in 1941, 138 Sqn expanded to 30 per month during 1942.

Losses sustained by 138 Sqn during 1942 included six Halifaxes and three Whitleys. Two of the former were bought down on October 29/30, when flown by Polish crews and assigned to Operation Wrench, during an SOE arms drop over Poland. Halifax W7773 was shot down in southern Norway with the loss of all seven on board; W7774 ditched off Sheringham, Norfolk, after receiving hits from a German night-fighter, but all were rescued by the local lifeboat.

A further loss just before Christmas 1942 – on December 22/23 – was Halifax II W7775 on another SOE operation to Holland. Six crew died, including the pilot, Flg Off Newport-Tinley DFC, in the crash near Meppel, two survivors becoming PoWs.

In February 1943, No 138 received its first Halifax II Series IA, while the previous month 161 Sqn sustained its first loss when DG285, flown by Plt Off H Readhead, an Australian, was lost on Operation Ker/Crab with all seven crew members near Rennes on the night of January 15/16. Whether due to flak or fighters remains unknown, but the aircraft was the first Halifax Mk V lost in action.

Gloom settled over both squadrons following operations on the night of March 14/15 when four Halifaxes failed to return to Tempsford. For 138 Sqn, BB281 had attempted to reach Czechoslovakia, but was shot down near Munich, while DT620 with Flt Sgt Smith in command was lost outbound over Denmark on a sortie to Poland. For 161 Sqn, DG245 was on an SIS mission with Flt Lt Prior DFM commanding, also to Czechoslovakia, but failed to return, while DG283 suffered engine failure on the way to France and crashed near Henley-on-Thames killing two of the six-man crew.

Mediterranean Missions

In March, four Halifaxes were transferred from Tempsford to north-west Africa for operations over Corsica and Sardinia. These supplemented the hard-pressed 148 Sqn which had existed as the Special Liberator Flight based at Gambut, Libya, but was now receiving Halifax II Series I and Series IAs. It had been criss-crossing the Mediterranean dropping agents and supplies to organisations in Greece, Crete, Serbia and Yugoslavia, but now with the Tempsford detachment based at Canrobert in Algeria and 148 Sqn further east, special ops ratcheted up to give greater support to the underground armies along the south of Europe.

Although enemy opposition was less intense than in northern Europe, operations from North Africa had their share of difficulties, not least being the harsh desert conditions, which made servicing aircraft in the open a nightmare for the ground crews. Even working long hours making the aircraft airworthy, losses were still sustained, sometimes due to engine failures, occasionally AA fire sought a victim, but often it was the weather which became the main enemy. Supply flights in the high mountainous regions of Greece and the Balkans where icing was an ever-present threat, claimed a number of machines.

In early-1944, the SOE squadrons began receiving Halifax Mk II or V Series IA versions to replace their ageing Series II (Special) machines and later, the SD squadrons began exchanging their aircraft for Stirlings, but not before the major effort to support the Warsaw uprising began on August 1, 1944. Both No 148 and 1586 Flight made great efforts to keep the Polish Home Army supplied with weapons and ammunition, but losses mounted as precision drops were attempted and often frustrated due to smoke and the indistinct front line.

On August 24, the Air Ministry requested up to ten Halifax Mk Vs from Bomber Command for supply to the Middle East with '… a minimum of 90 hours to go before the next major inspection; must be operationally serviceable and fitted out to full SD standard.' These were ferried out to Brindisi within 48hr and a further eight followed, but some of the latter were found to have unreliable Merlin XX engines instead of improved 22s and could not be used. By the end of September, the Polish forces had surrendered with heavy casualties.

The end in sight

In August 1944, No 138 Sqn finally lost its much-used Halifax equipment as Short Stirlings took over the Special Duty role at Tempsford. Co-located No 161 Sqn relinquished its Halifax Vs in October as Stirling IVs arrived, while in the Middle East, the experienced Polish-manned 1586 Flight had reached full squadron status and became 301 (SD) Sqn retaining Halifax IIs and Vs with some Liberators until March 1945. No 148 Sqn in Italy also kept its Halifaxes, flying them on Partisan supply missions in Yugoslavia until May 1945 when they were finally withdrawn.

While Bomber Command found much to criticise about the Halifax in the early years, the aircraft proved its worth as a long-range special duties machine, virtually from its first operational missions. For the SD role, it carried agents and equipment to the farthest reaches of Europe and while its weaknesses affected all its users, it had the range and capability to help 'set Europe ablaze'.

Air drop containers and packages being prepared and loaded into a 148 Sqn B.II of the Balkan Air Force for a night supply operation in support of Yugoslav partisans. The date was October 1944, and the aircraft was BB338 which crashed in the sea the following month on another supply drop. (via *Aeroplane*)

Chapter 10

Tugging with the Airborne Forces

On November 19, 1942, two Halifax-Horsa combinations took off from Skitten airfield in Scotland bound for a Commando attack on the German Norsk Hydro heavy water plant at Vermok, Norway. Code-named Operation *Freshman*, it sadly proved unsuccessful. The first aircraft crash-landed in a hill with loss or injury to all, while the second aircraft failed to locate the landing area and elected to return to Scotland. However, the tow line parted and the Horsa crashed. Those who hadn't died in the landing were subsequently executed by the Germans on the direct orders of Hitler.

For the Halifax in the Airborne Forces role this was an inauspicious start, but the type proved its worth during later operations such as the invasions of Sicily and Normandy, as well as the crossing of the Rhine.

A Halifax at full power pulls an Airspeed Horsa Mk II glider off the ground on a re-supply mission to France after D-Day. Early experience called for the tug to be flown with consideration for the glider pilot and it was also considered of benefit if the tug pilots could do some glider flying themselves, thereby understanding some of the problems of those controlling the Horsas. Normal maximum towing speed for both the Horsa and the much larger Hamilcar was a modest 150mph. (via *Aeroplane*)

An oft-published picture, but one that illustrates Operation *Mallard*, the heavy glider commitment during the D-Day invasion. Two Horsas head the lines ready to be towed off and behind these are 30 General Aircraft Hamilcar heavy transport gliders loaded with jeeps, 17-pounder anti-tank guns, trailers and stores to hold and expand the Normandy beachhead. Either side of the Tarrant Rushton runway are the 32 Halifax Mk V tugs of 298 and 644 Sqn, which in turn will pull the 15.5-ton Hamilcars off and over the Channel. In addition, each Halifax carried nine equipment containers which were dropped in the landing zone. All aircraft taking part in D-Day wore black and white stripes applied the evening before. (via Barry Charles Wheeler)

In October 1941, five months from the spectacular if flawed German airborne operation to capture the island of Crete, Halifax B.II Series I R9435 arrived with the Airborne Forces Development Unit at Ringway to begin trials on carrying and dropping paratroops. For this, a hatch was cut in the fuselage floor. Then in January 1942, now fitted with a towing pylon under the tail, it undertook flights at Snaith in Yorkshire, with the new Airspeed Horsa troop-carrying glider, followed a month later by the first Halifax-Hamilcar tank-carrying glider flight from Newmarket Heath.

By June, seven Halifaxes were employed in towing and training with gliders; No 38 Wing Army Co-operation Command was formed the same month for the express purpose of honing plans for the deployment of British airborne troops. Rootes built 30 Halifax A.IIIs and Handley Page's Rawcliffe Repair Depot turned out a batch of interim Halifax A.VIIs which had the dorsal turret deleted, a glider-towing attachment fitted and seating for 12 paratroops in the fuselage. Aircraft were fitted with either 12ft 9in or 13ft diameter propellers and some flew with a combination of three and four-blade props.

Towing gliders was very much a team effort and many tug crews made a point of getting to know the glider pilots and their Army charges. The basics of the operation involved particular care on behalf of the tug pilot. Having hitched up the glider's tow cable, the Halifax prepared for take-off by inching forward until the cable was taut. The tug pilot slowly applied power and the two aircraft gathered speed. The glider was airborne first at about 65 knots and assumed the 'high tow' position and helped pull the Halifax tail up. Take-off took about 45sec. Climbing away with the glider higher than the tug, the two machines cruised at around 130 knots, with the tug pilot keeping a sharp eye on the all-important engine temperatures as the load was considerable and an engine failure meant a quick decision on whether the glider should cast off!

An intercom connection ran down the centre of the tow cable to maintain contact between the two aircraft and it was an unwritten law among the glider-towing crews that no matter what the emergency was, it was the glider pilot who had to make the decision to cast-off! The well-being of the glider and troops took precedence over the Halifax crew.

Ferry to Sicily

No 295 Sqn was formed at Netheravon, first with Whitleys and from February 1943 with Halifax Vs. Transferring to Holmsley South in the New Forest, the squadron was tasked with ferrying 36 Horsa gliders from the UK to Tunisia in June 1943 preparatory to their use for Operation Beggar as part of the invasion of Sicily in July. The squadron employed A Flight with 12 Halifaxes for the task

The ferry journey was divided into three stages. The first, Portreath across the Bay of Biscay and around Portugal to Sale, near Rabat in Morocco, was some 1,200 miles; the second covered Sale to Froha near Mascara, and the third, from Froha to Kairouan, totalling a further 1,000 miles. Only 26 Horsas and eight Halifaxes eventually arrived at Sale for the second part of their journey and with more losses en route, the force was further depleted. Five Halifaxes required engine changes, mostly due to oil leaks.

The practicalities of a Halifax-Horsa combination were highlighted in a report submitted by Flt Lt DA Grant, a pilot on 295 Sqn, after the Sicily operation. He noted that tows over 1,000 miles were unwise, given the high fuel load of the Halifax and the vibration and wear on the airframe and engines; if such distances were to be flown, the tug should be in tip-top condition. Engine failures, often due to oil or coolant leaks, were the biggest problem and where aircraft were lost without trace, it was believed that this was probably the main cause, rather than enemy action.

On the actual airborne assault, of the eight Horsas due to land, capture and hold a bridge until relieved by the Allied invasion force, only the one towed by Grant achieved its goal. The troops held the bridge until their ammunition ran out, forcing the small British force to surrender to the Italians (only to be released very shortly afterwards when the Eighth Army arrived). Of the other Horsas, two were missing, a third was prematurely released due to a tow rope break, the fourth crashed into the canal bank killing the crew, and the other three landed about two miles short of the target.

By March 1944, Halifax A.III and A.VII tugs were in service with two squadrons, No 298 and 644 within No 38 Wing. The former was assigned to tow the Hamilcar while the latter had perfected the precision landing of Horsas and it was this combination that initiated the invasion of Normandy on June 6, 1944, with landings successfully achieved close to the vital bridges over the Orne and Caen canals.

Both squadrons were involved in the ill-fated landings at Arnhem – Operation Market Garden – in September 1944, and with the newly converted 296 Sqn which received Halifax Vs and IIIs in place of Albemarles, they participated in Operation Varsity, the Rhine crossing in March 1945. For this, the Allies used a massive force of 1,795 gliders of which 440 were Horsas and Hamilcars supported by American Waco Hadrians, tugged by 1,305 aircraft. Over 21,000 airborne troops were flown in for this, the final airborne operation of the war.

The Halifax A.VII was also equipped to drop a Jeep and 6pdr gun from a main heavy-duty beam in the bomb-bay, the aim being to give the airborne troops greater mobility once on the ground; some of these combinations were also dropped on D-Day.

Halifax A.IX for the Airborne

To follow the A.VII, HP developed the A.IX as a special conversion of the Halifax VI for use by the Airborne Forces. Designated HP.71, the design work for what would be the last production version of the Halifax was sub-contracted to Boulton-Paul at Wolverhampton. Powered by four 1,675hp Hercules XVI engines, the 'new' design appeared to have scarcely altered from earlier types, but incorporated most of the changes internally to reflect its troop-carrying role with folding seats for 16 paratroops (eight a side aft of the rear spar) and two dispatchers, a new inward-opening paratroop door, a heating system to give a modicum of luxury to the troops as well as the crew, and a Boulton-Paul type D rear turret mounting two 0.5in Browning machine-guns for self-defence. As well as a retractable tailwheel and glider-towing hook, an equipment pannier or additional range-extending fuel tanks could be carried in the bomb-bay. The dorsal turret was deleted, and the crew reduced to six.

For development work, Halifax LV999/G was used and production of the A.IX began at Cricklewood with batch RT758-RT799. The first aircraft off the line, RT758, was delivered to the Airborne Forces Experimental Establishment on October 23, 1945, followed by two more in November. With the end of the war, only 145 A.IXs were built, most going straight in to store, but some were flown out to Aqir and Qastina in Palestine in August 1946 to supplement A.VIIs with No 620 and 644 Sqns.

However, their service use was brief, the former being renumbered 113 Sqn before disbanding in April 1947, while the latter became 47 Sqn and retained its A.IXs until it returned to RAF Fairford, relinquishing them in September '48 when the first Hastings arrived. No 297 at Brize Norton received A.IXs in January '47, hanging on to them until October the following year when they too left for storage and breaking up.

Seen from under the wings of the Hamilcars, the Halifax Vs await start-up. (via Barry Charles Wheeler)

Chapter 11

Halifax – The Electronic Support Club

Electronic warfare moved centre stage as the bomber battle entered its final, climactic end. The German electronics industry, led by companies like Telefunken and Siemens worked hard to give the Luftwaffe night-fighter force radar equipment to detect and destroy their prey and in turn, 'boffins' at the Radio Warfare Establishment at Watton and others at Farnborough were as tenacious at finding suitable countermeasures to protect the nocturnal force in its grim task of destroying Hitler's war machine.

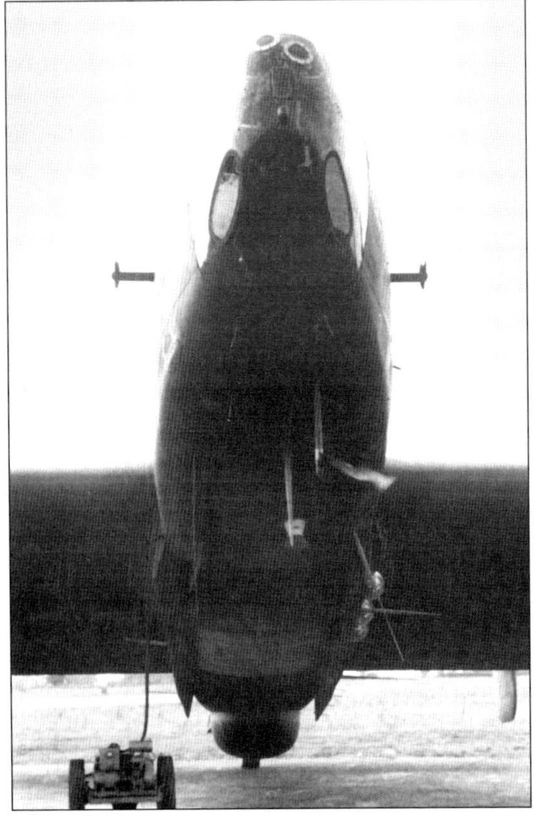

A view of the underside of a 462 Sqn B.III showing the 'Mandrel' jamming aerials, the forward one located behind the front pitot tube. In the rear of the bomb-bay is an additional fuel tank and either side of the nose are aerials for the Rebecca system. The three small round fairings on the side of the open bomb-bay door could be Carpet RCM aerials. (M Wright)

On November 23, 1943, RAF Bomber Command formed No 100 Group as a secret support arm under the overall command of Air Vice Marshal EB Addison. In addition to some select squadrons of Mosquitos, the new group also found a vital task for the Halifax which gained unexpected recognition as the aircraft of choice to carry within its capacious fuselage the plethora of 'black boxes' and equipment as well as additional crewmen to undertake the expanding role of radio countermeasures (RCM) to confuse and eventually defeat the enemy.

One of the first flying elements within 100 Group was the Bomber Support Development Unit established at Foulsham in April 1944 before moving to Swanton Morley in December. Its first aircraft was a prototype 'jamming' Halifax fitted with a range of transmitter/receivers including Airborne Cigar and Carpet II/IIIs, externally identified by the distinctive masts and extra antennae along the fuselage top. Two more aircraft followed, one with a Loran navigation aid and the other with four Airborne Grocer IIs to jam Wurzburg ground-control intercept radars, as well as Carpet and TR.1143A transmitter/receivers.

Absorbed into the Group was No 1473 Flight which had been on RCM duties since mid 1942 and in January 1944 became part of 192 Sqn flying a single Halifax B.II Srs I (Special), DT735 on electronic intelligence (Elint) duties. Other squadrons flying RCM missions were No 171 (coded 6Y) which took on Halifax B.IIIs in late-1944, dropping Window as part of the Special Window

One role in which the Halifax excelled was that of radio countermeasures or RCM, its roomy interior allowing installation of the various 'black boxes' needed to confuse and defeat the enemy's radar and radio transmissions. No 462 RAAF Sqn at Foulsham became part of 100 (Bomber Support) Group at the beginning of 1945 and specialised in operations with B.IIIs fitted with 'Airborne Cigar' (ABC). The two transmitting aerials for ABC on this 462 Sqn aircraft are forward of the mid-upper turret and just visible in the original photograph are four whip aerials for receiving signals between the mid and rear turrets. A chaff or 'Window' dropping chute is just behind the ventral H2S bulge and below the R-Roger letter. The 'Monica' tail warning aerial is below the tail turret. (via Barry Charles Wheeler)

Force and jamming radars with Mandrel, No 192 (coded DT) which was formerly Wellington-equipped and received Halifax B.IIIs in November 1943, No 199 Sqn (coded EX) which converted from Stirlings to Halifaxes in February 1945 and undertook Window and Mandrel sorties, and No 462 RAAF Sqn (coded Z5) at Foulsham which was the last squadron to join 100 Group and just managed to begin full-scale jamming missions with Airborne Cigar, Carpet and Piperack, as well as Window, in March 1945 before disbanding in September that year.

The final unit within 100 Group was No 1341 Flight formed at East Kirkby on December 21, 1944, for Elint duties in the Far East. Five Halifax B.IIIs fitted with additional fuel tanks in the bomb-bay flew to Digri airfield in India and operated from the beginning of June 1945. Amalgamated with C Flt of 159 Sqn, the unit operated only a small number of sorties in its designated role before Japan surrendered in August. It subsequently operated on ferry duties to Kunming in China and dropped supplies to PoW camps before disbanding in October 1945.

Withdrawn and languishing in a graveyard at York on Boxing Day 1945, this 462 Sqn ABC-equipped Halifax B.III is PN451/G. The incomplete tail stripes are yellow. (via Barry Charles Wheeler)

Jamming & Elint equipment

Airborne Cigar or ABC – VHF R/T jammer which produced a warbling note to jam enemy radio transmissions.

Carpet – transmitter to jam Wurzburg fire-control radar.

Jostle – high-powered transmitter radiating noise on German fighter control channels.

Mandrel – operated by additional crewman to jam frequencies used by Freya, Mammut and Wassermann radars. Used T.1408A/E transmitter, Type 68 modulator, Type 300 power unit and VHF aerial. Later Mandrel units covered other radar frequencies.

Piperack – jammed SN-2 airborne radar frequencies.

Window – strips of aluminium foil 30cm in length and 1.5cm wide to 'blind' search radars.

Chapter 12

Heavy Colours

When the Halifax began joining RAF squadrons in 1941, night bomber camouflage had been standardised as Dark Green and Dark Earth colours applied in a disruptive pattern over all top surfaces, and non-reflective Special Night (black) finish on the sides and undersides of the wings, tail and fuselage. These dull matt colours applied to the early production Halifax B.Is and IIs. The demarcation between the top surface colours and the Special Night was by way of a wavy line roughly mid-way up the fuselage sides.

Serials on the rear upper fuselage were Dull Red and the code letters were Dark Grey, later changed to Medium Grey before adopting Dull Red throughout the Command. In mid-1941, the Night areas were further extended up the fuselage, terminating in a wavy line between the cockpit canopy and the leading edge of the tailplane. This changed again as production increased to mostly a straight demarcation line.

National markings were matt Red and Blue Type B roundels only on the upper wings (applied on night bombers 1923–47); Red, White, Blue, Yellow Type A.1 roundels on the fuselage sides until June 1942; modified Red, White, Blue, Yellow Type C roundels on the fuselage sides 1942–47. Fin flash – Red, White, Blue in equal division of colours with Red leading until June 1942; modified dimensions from June 1942–47.

An exception to the standard RAF markings was the adoption of French roundels on the fuselage sides of the two Free French Halifax squadrons, No 346 'Guyenne' and 347 'Tunisie' based at Elvington in 1944–45.

Plan View Concealment

The top surface disruptive camouflage pattern colours on Halifaxes were initially applied in alternate A and B designs, but during 1941 the A pattern was applied as standard to speed production. When Halifax bombers were hastily transferred to the Middle East in mid-1942, they received an upper surface colour of Middle Stone over the Dark Green, while retaining the Dark Earth and their lower Night finish.

An early Halifax B.I L9515 fitted with Merlin XX engines and converted to a Mk II for trials at Boscombe Down. The wavy demarcation between the black undersurfaces and the green and brown camouflage uppersurfaces was a feature of early production aircraft. (via Barry Charles Wheeler)

An English Electric Halifax B.II with the final shape fins. Stencilled on the rudder and fin are the EE part numbers. Projecting below the rear turret is the Monica tail warning device. (via Barry Charles Wheeler)

From 1942, Bomber Command Halifaxes began appearing in a smooth Night colour to replace the rough matt finish in one of a number of moves to try and increase performance. Later in the war, squadrons flying the much improved Halifax B.III were ordered to apply broad coloured bands of various designs on the fin and rudders of their aircraft to better identify aircraft from the various Halifax-equipped Groups.

Quite a number of bombers carried unofficial markings and bombing scores on the fuselage sides below the cockpit, but there were more without these embellishments than with them. Those that were painted were usually the result of a discussion between the crew as to the design and when agreed, a talented member of the ground crew undertook the painting using what colours were available from stores. Sometimes, turret gunners painted their successes, usually in the form of swastikas, close to their turrets.

Post-war, the Halifax was quickly retired from military service. Those few that remained in use were to be seen retaining their wartime colours, often with their serials painted white in large letters and numbers under the outboard wings. As the former RAF aircraft were quickly snapped up by small independent airlines, so their military paint was removed during conversion and natural metal skins shone as commercial names and civil identities appeared for the first time on the former night-bombing airframes.

Within a short time, Handley Page had changed the colour application to a straight line along most of the fuselage. Later, other companies further raised the line to reduce the camouflage to a small, thin area along the top.
(via Barry Charles Wheeler)

Top view of a London Passenger-built B.II, with one of the two applied camouflage patterns.
(via Barry Charles Wheeler)

Coastal Colours

Halifaxes joining RAF Coastal Command exchanged their night camouflage for a scheme more in keeping with their over-water operations. Early in February 1943, the Command ordered that general reconnaissance aircraft, such as the Halifax and other four-engined types like the Sunderland flying-boat, would be given a white finish on all surfaces, leaving only the strict plan view in a temperate sea scheme of Extra Dark Sea Grey and Dark Slate Grey. This was to reduce the chance of being spotted at long range by the U-boat crews and allow the RAF patroller to approach the surfaced submarine before it dived and escaped attack.

The new layout replaced the earlier colouring in which the sea scheme extended down the sides to meet the grey under-surfaces. Henceforth, the white was applied in a dull matt finish to all front areas including engine cowlings and propeller spinners while the undersides of the wings, tail and fuselage would be given gloss white.The upper surfaces would be Dark Sea Grey overall. Serials were marked in Light Slate Grey and codes in Red.

Later in 1943, Coastal Command patrol squadrons were ordered to apply Extra Dark Sea Grey to the top surface of all aircraft and this remained in use until the end of the war.

This London Passenger Transport-built B.II at Leavesden was pictured in October 1943 and shows girls working on the upper surface. The camouflage pattern shows the alternative scheme with the colours reversed. (via Philip Jarrett)

Chapter 13

Halifax in Foreign Military Hands

Armée de l'Air Halifaxes

France began its association with the Handley Page Halifax following the establishment of 'Free French' squadrons in Britain in 1940, initially with Spitfires and later with Boston light bombers. In 1944, personnel who had experience on the twin-engine Loire et Olivier 451 bomber in the Middle East were brought together in England to form two heavy bomber squadrons equipped with Handley Page Halifaxes.

Established with RAF help, the two squadrons were No 346 Guyenne Sqn and 347 Tunisie Sqn assigned as part of No 4 Group based at Elvington, near the ancient town of York. The French crews undertook refresher training at No 20 (Wellington) Operational Training Unit at Lossiemouth followed by a short familiarisation course at Driffield on early mark Halifaxes. On May 16, 1944, 346 Guyenne Sqn assembled at their new airfield under the command of Lt Col GE Venot.

French Halifax crews served with distinction over the last year of the European war and as part of the British effort to help resurrect the 'new' post-war Armée de l'Air, the two Bomber Command squadrons, No 346 and 347 Sqn disbanded, but the crews with their aircraft returned to France to form a bomber-transport wing. This former 346 Guyenne Sqn Halifax III is taking part in the July 14 celebration fly-past over Paris in 1947 with fin flashes in French national colours and Type C roundels on the wings. (via Barry Charles Wheeler)

The squadron was allocated an establishment of 20 Halifax B.Vs, 16 in use with four in reserve and after working up on their new charges, the squadron was declared operational. Proudly carrying French blue-white-red roundels on the sides of its new aircraft, the squadron set out on its first mission on June 1/2, 1944, an attack on a German radio-listening station at Ferme-d'Urville. The French squadron contributed 12 aircraft to a total force of 101 Halifaxes, bombing on the coloured markers. Unfortunately, the results were frustrated by cloud and haze, each aircraft dropping five 1,000lb and ten 500lb bombs.

On June 20, 1944, No 347 Tunisie Sqn was formed at Elvington, under the command of Lt Col M Vigouroux. After a spell on local training flights it joined its sister squadron Guyenne on operations from June 27/28 when 12 aircraft took off to bomb Mont Candon, dropping 175 500lb bombs on the target.

At the end of June, Halifax B.IIIs arrived to replace the B.Vs with 346 Sqn and at the end of July, No 347 followed suite. Through August the targets were V1 sites and support for the Allied forces in Normandy and in September, both squadrons assisted with the transport of fuel to Melsbroek, Brussels, to keep the armoured units mobile in their on-going pursuit of the enemy. Bomber Command returned to its night offensive against German targets in October and both French squadrons took part in attacks, notably against Heligoland in daylight on April 18, 1945.

Seven days later, both 346 and 347 Sqns, now flying B.VIs, flew their last attack of the war when the gun batteries on the island of Wangerooge were bombed in daylight causing heavy damage. Over the following days and after the end of hostilities, the crews conducted a series of training and support duties, including dumping stocks of unwanted bombs into the sea, and communication flights to and from France.

On October 6, 1945, after flying with the RAF for 11 months and making 1,479 sorties, No 346 Guyenne Sqn transferred to the French Air Force. Its sister unit, No 347 Tunisie Sqn transferred in November after ten months and 1,355 sorties with Bomber Command. By the end of October, the two squadrons had returned home.

Coded L8-H for No 347 Tunisie Sqn, RG867 was a new-build B.VI from English Electric and was delivered in August 1945, passing to the French via No 1 Ferry Unit. In Armée de l'Air use, the Halifaxes were generally unarmed but maintained their bomber role with the additional tasks of transport, meteorological and search and rescue duties. (via Barry Charles Wheeler)

In France, a revitalised Armée de l'Air incorporated the two Halifax squadrons into its Groupes de Bombardement as GB.II/23 Guyenne and GB.I/25 Tunisie, based at Bordeaux-Marignac. To maintain serviceability on their B.VIs, the French requested and received from the RAF at least four Halifax B.IIs and Vs for ground training at Rochefort.

The two squadrons undertook a number of different duties, GB.I/25 flew met flights and SAR missions, while GB.II/23 was tasked with long-range transport for which their aircraft were modified with seating for up to 20 passengers. Flights were made to Algeria and Tunisia, and later to Indo-China and France's far-flung outposts across the Pacific, and to South America on diplomatic and casualty relief work. The strength of the French Halifax units was around 31 aircraft in 1947 and another batch of 14 surplus RAF B.VIs arrived by October.

Bastille Day July 14, 1948, was the last appearance of the Halifax in public when five took part in a fly-past over Paris. The type was officially withdrawn from air force use in October 1951, but some continued to fly on experimental work with organisations such as the Centre d'Essais en Vol (CEV) at Bretigny and Istres. The final Halifaxes, believed to be RG703 and RG828, conducted air tests with missiles until the spring of 1953, long outlasting the type in RAF service which all but consigned its bomber fleet to the scrap-man.

Halifaxes known to carry French colours include the following: JP327, JN978, LL392, LL467, PP165, RG491, RG500, RG510, RG562, RG590, RG605, RG606, RG607, RG625, RG645, RG647, RG653, RG655, RG661, RG670, RG703, RG705, RG752, RG788, RG798, RG816, RG819, RG821, RG828, RG867, RG868, RG869, RG874, ST797, ST799, and ST800.

For French civil operators, see under Civil Halifaxes.

Royal Egyptian Air Force
See entry in Civil Halifaxes.

Royal Pakistan Air Force
Following partition in July 1947, the Dominion of Pakistan was formally constituted and established an air force. As well as a handful of mostly unserviceable Hawker Tempest fighters and some Douglas Dakota transports, the fledgling Royal Pakistan Air Force looked around for a bomber type to form an offensive element should one of Pakistan's neighbours decide to mount a 'foreign venture' against the new state.

The Halifax B.VI was available from the many stored former-RAF examples following the war, and the Pakistan purchasing team, under RAF liaison officer guidance, bought eight to form a bomber squadron. Flown from Stansted to Thame airfield for overhaul by Airtech Ltd, the aircraft were modified to each carry spare Hercules engines in the bomb bay. Five had seen no RAF service and had been acquired by London Aero Motors Service. In October 1949, the eight aircraft were ferried out by British-American Air Service crews to Pakistan and on arrival at Mauripur, Karachi, formed No 12 Sqn RPAF.

In service, the Halifaxes were stripped of their former wartime camouflage and operated in bare metal finish on reconnaissance and transport duties. To supplement the fleet, three civilianised C.VIIIs were purchased and ferried from Britain in May 1948, of which AP-ABZ (ex-PP312) force-landed near Shaibah through lack of fuel. The two surviving C.VIIIs, AP-ACH and 'ACG were flown by Pak-Air Ltd and ended their days as instructional airframes until the Halifax VIs were withdrawn in 1955.

RPAF Halifax B.VIs: G-AJBE (RG785); G-AKAW (RG784); G-AKLI (RG783); G-AKLJ (RG781); G-AKLK (RG779); RG782 (unregistered). RPAF Halifax C.VIIIs: G-AJNU (PP279) to AP-ACH; G-AJNX (PP312) to AP-ABZ; G-AJNY (PP322) to AP-ACG).

Above: This stunning shot shows two 346 Guyenne Sqn B.VIs, still sporting their RAF codes but repainted with French national roundels and blue-white-red rudder stripes. These originated from a batch of 300 built by the English Electric Company – considered by RAF crews to be the highest-quality Halifaxes built – and both carry 8,000lb freight panniers in the bomb bays. (via Barry Charles Wheeler)

Left: A cold winter's day at Elvington bomber base, Yorkshire, and the bearded Capitaine Marchal of No 346 Guyenne chats with his crew in December 1944. All wear standard RAF flight gear, but retain French badges on their berets. Marchal's Halifax B.III is H7-Q LL553 and carries the Free French Cross of Lorraine in front of the badge. Under the cockpit are 47 bomb symbols and a single German cross signifying the success of one of the turret gunners. The lower markings are eight petrol cans recording the number of urgent fuel supply flights flown by the aircraft between September 15 and October 2, 1944, to Brussels Melsbroek for the Allied ground forces. (ECPA via Barry Charles Wheeler)

Right: Nose art on Capt Marchal's aircraft. Painted by a member of the ground crew, it represents the statue of the departure of the volunteers by François Rude on the Arc de Triomphe in Paris.

Below: French ground crew load a 2,000lb bomb, suitably marked, into the bomb bay of a Halifax at Elvington in winter 1944. (ECPA via Barry Charles Wheeler)

Among a number of C.VIIIs converted to civilian use was PP287 which received the registration G-AGPC. In October 1947, it transferred to the French register as F-BCJS with Aero Cargo at Lyons with which it operated for a year, crashing on take-off at Lyons-Bron in December 1948 on its way to Casablanca. (via M Hooks)

One of the nine Halifax A.IXs delivered of 12 purchased by the Egyptian Air Force. Converted by Aviation Traders as G-ALVK, it became 1160 in EAF service. (via Barry Charles Wheeler)

Top, middle and right:
Six of eight Halifax B.VIs for Pakistan are pictured in these views taken at Thame airfield where Airtech Ltd undertook the conversion work. The aircraft were modified to ferry spare Hercules engines on their trip to Asia, the powerplant hanging suspended in a cradle from the bomb-bay. Following delivery in 1949, the bombers equipped No 12 Sqn of the newly formed Royal Pakistan Air Force. (via *Aeroplane*)

Chapter 14

Halifax Transports – Civil and Military

I n 1943, a Super-Halifax design was put forward by Handley Page to the Ministry of Aircraft Production. Among a range of refinements, the company-designated HP.65 would have a 3,000-mile range, new low-drag high-aspect ratio wings, twin main wheels, and turbo-supercharged Bristol Hercules 38 engines. However, to the disappointment of the company, it produced no interest from the MAP, but what did elicit a positive response some months later was a transport development of the existing bomber which was offered in December 1943 as the HP.64.

This was developed on a low-priority basis, emerging as the Transport A (a stripped Halifax III, VI or VII bomber) and the Transport B which incorporated a ventral pannier of 8,000lb capacity in place of the bomb doors. In February 1945, the pannier was flight-tested and 100 new Halifax C.VIIIs, powered by four 1,675hp Hercules 100 engines, were ordered under the company number HP.70; 304 panniers were also ordered.

Transport versions of the Halifax were developed from the bomber, the first being the C.III with seating for eight passengers and most saw deletion of the H2S scanner, the dorsal turret and Monica tail radar. The A.VII, seen here, was a later design for No 38 Group for use by Airborne Forces. A glider towing hook was fitted as standard and up to 12 paratroops were accommodated. This example, PN261/R was flown by 298 Sqn. (via Barry Charles Wheeler)

The need for a high-capacity freighter was met by the C.VIII which could be fitted with an 8,000lb pannier in place of the original bomb-bay. Given the new type designation HP.70, the prototype PP225 flew in June 1945. These two views show PP310 with the new tail cone, but without the pannier. (via Barry Charles Wheeler)

The new variant had a crew of five including two pilots and dual controls, and the cleaned-up main fuselage interior could accommodate ten stretchers or 11 passengers. The prototype, PP225, flew in June 1945 and production aircraft were issued to the two Polish-manned squadrons, No 301 and 304 based at Chedburgh.

Most of the Halifax C.VIIIs were delivered straight into store and were joined by the few in-service examples when they were retired from RAF use after just a year through 1946. With so many military aircraft now stored after Service use, civil operators were quick to buy those types they considered commercially viable, often at around £2,000 each, before more modern airliner designs arrived on the market.

The recently-built Halifax C.VIII was near the top of the list and 90 received British civil registrations. Among the first to acquire the type was London Aero and Motor Services Ltd at Elstree which bought six of an eventual 16 for freight operations. Fitted with the 8,000lb capacity ventral pannier, the blue-painted LAMS Halifaxes were soon employed flying fresh fruit from Italy and southern France to a Britain which was still undergoing stringent rationing with fruit a rarity. Sadly, LAMS founder, Dr Graham Humby, fell ill in December 1947 and in spite of the company's European

A silver-finished Halifax was an unusual sight in 1945, but C.VIII PP285 was retained by Handley Page as a demonstrator. With its freight pannier, rounded tail cone and unwarlike appearance, this former warhorse appears rather handsome. (via Barry Charles Wheeler)

contracts and 'tramping' in Australasia and Africa, trading came to a halt in July 1948, only two years after its formation.

Other British commercial operators of the C.VIII included Air Freight (four), Bond Air Services with a fleet of 14 which included two A.IXs and Haltons, British American Air Services (six), Eagle Aviation (six), Lancashire Aircraft Corporation at Squires Gate (45, of which 27 never entered service), Skyflight (five) and Westminster Airways (four).

Only two Halifax A.IXs were fully civilianised, G-ALON and 'LOS, this task being undertaken by Aviation Traders Ltd at Southend. Both were operated by Bond Air Services and the second aircraft, serial RT937, flew 161 sorties on the Berlin Airlift.

Haltons with BOAC

The only version of the Halifax which came anywhere near being an airliner was the Halton, a post-war rework for British Overseas Airways Corporation to help bridge the gap caused by late delivery of the new Avro Tudor II. To give BOAC crews some experience of the Halifax, three C.VIIIs were loaned to the airline by Handley Page in October 1945 to fly mail services between Bournemouth's Hurn Airport and the Gold Coast city of Accra. This proved surprisingly successful and 12 aircraft, all C.VIIIs and given the fleet name Halton, were built at Radlett and flown to Short Brothers at Belfast for fitting-out to BOAC requirements.

Each aircraft was equipped with the belly pannier and a large entrance door was located in the starboard side of the fuselage. Inside the narrow main cabin, a galley, toilet and ten blue-covered passenger seats were installed, while rust-coloured curtains hung at the large windows fitted adjacent to each of the seats.

The prototype G-AHDU was christened by Lady Winster, wife of the then Minister of Civil Aviation, at Radlett on July 18, 1946, and given the name *Falkirk*. It flew a 7,000-mile proving flight to Khartoum later that month and by September, six Haltons had been delivered to the BOAC base at Bovingdon to operate the service to Cairo.

Unfortunately, some of the trouble that had beset the Halifax in the past returned to plague the new aircraft during its first month of operations – among them was a lack of adequate de-icing equipment and hydraulic system failures. Frustrated, not least due to the cost of the conversions, the airline returned the first six aircraft to HP for the problems to be rectified.

Nine months later, on June 2, 1947, the Haltons returned to the Cairo route, followed later by London-Lagos via Casablanca, Dakar and Accra. Other services were flown to Colombo via Cairo, Basra and Karachi, for a single fare of £148. Just under a year later, the final Halton service was flown on May 4, 1948, the Accra-Heathrow flight terminating the type's stop-gap operation with Britain's flag-carrier.

Egyptian Halifaxes

On withdrawal from service, one aircraft was bought by the French Louis Breguet company (G-AHDR *Foreland*), while the other11 went to Aviation Traders at Southend where they joined 32 Halifax A.IXs granted civilian status for onward transfer to other operators, one of which was the Royal Egyptian Air Force. The REAF purchased nine with the first aircraft flying out to Cairo, via Malta, in January 1949. Interestingly, among the nine was G-ALVM, formerly RT938 and the 6,176th and last Halifax built.

In the then Royal Egyptian Air Force they were given REAF serials 1155 (ex G-ALOP), 1156 ('VI), 1157 ('OR), 1158 ('OO), 1159 ('VJ), 1160 ('VK), 1161 ('VM), 1162 ('VL) and 1163 ('VH). All had been stripped of armament before delivery, but the Egyptians fitted machine guns in an attempt to give them some self-protection. Interestingly, these A.IXs joined three C.VIIIs already acquired by the REAF. They were former Swiss aircraft from Air Globe of Geneva registered HB-AIF, 'AIL and 'AIM. The Halifaxes were mostly used for transport duties, but with an embargo on British equipment

Two Polish-manned RAF squadrons took delivery of C.VIIIs and made a brave attempt at flying the type during 1946. However, both were disbanded at the end of that year and the aircraft withdrawn from service. PP329 of 301 Sqn, with the Polish badge on the nose, has its pannier in place, but with no rudders it looks ready for the scrapman. It survived however, to fly with LAMS in 1947 as G-AKIE. (Richard Riding)

due to Egypt's attack on the new Jewish state, spares became a constant requirement and the less able examples were cannibalised to keep the dwindling force flying. The remaining few were destroyed in air attacks during the Suez invasion of 1956.

Commercially French

There were only three civil users of the HP Halifax in France in the immediate post-war years, SOCOTRA, SANA and Aerocargo. The first was Société Co-opérative de Transport Aérien which bought F-BCJZ, a C.VIII, on October 22, 1947. Previously G-AJBK of Air Freight Ltd, it was flown by SOCOTRA on cargo contracts.

SANA (Société Auxiliaire de Navigation Aérienne) received F-BCJQ, 'CJR (delivered in June 1947), 'CJT (del in October '47) and 'ESE (del in June '48 and damaged by fire in '49). Most had been withdrawn from use by 1951.

Operating from Casablanca and Lyon, Aerocargo received F-BCJS in late 1948, 'CJV, 'CJX and 'ECK, using them as freighters for ad hoc flights around the French colonies and mainland France.

Halifax in Switzerland

Three C.VIIIs were bought by Air Globe, based in Cointrin, Geneva, and delivered from late-1947. Registered HB-AIF, 'AIK, and 'AIL, they were operated for just over a year in the transport role before being sold to the Royal Egyptian Air Force in December 1948. A fourth aircraft, HB-AIM was not delivered to Air Globe, returning to its UK registration G-AKBR.

From Bombers to Saviours – Halifaxes return to Berlin

With the closing of surface access to Berlin by the occupying Soviet forces on June 24, 1948, the other three powers, Britain, France and the USA, initiated one of the greatest airlifts of the age! Operation Plainfare saw the RAF, flying supplies from West German bases to the Berlin airfield of Gatow. One month into the lifeline, it was clear that the RAF force of Dakotas and Yorks would not be able to supply all that the city's population required to survive the blockade.

To augment the RAF fleet, British air charter companies were called upon and from the start of the combined military/civil airlift on August 4, the Halifax proved itself to be the most successful of all the civil types used by the British over the year-long supply operation. Seven companies operated a total of 38 Halifax C.VIII/Haltons and two A.IXs over the following 12 months and the first to fly a sortie was Bond Air Services' G-AIOI from Wunstorf to Gatow on the opening night, piloted by Capt Treen – appropriate, given the type's earlier wartime role – of August 4, followed by a further four sorties within that first 24hr period. Bond operated 12 Haltons on the airlift and 'IOI went on to complete 129 sorties before being written-off in an accident at Tegel on February 15, 1949.

While the Halifax could carry more cargo and foodstuffs than the RAF Dakotas and Yorks, given its large capacity bomb bay it was considered ideal for conversion into a tanker role and Airtech at Thame converted G-AKBB and 'KGN for the carriage of fuel oil. However, having pumped 'KBB full of oil at Schleswigland for a flight to Berlin on February 11, 1949, the main gear failed to retract and during the subsequent emergency landing, the heavy fuel oil which took the normal landing weight

The war is over, but Handley Page still had contracts to fulfil, one of which was for 146 A.IXs for 38 Group Airborne Forces. An improved A.VII with seating for up to 16 paratroops and retaining the rear turret, now fitted with two 0.50in guns, the A.IX served briefly with RAF squadrons before retirement. Egypt requested 12, but only nine arrived and the last ceased flying around the time of the Suez crisis in 1956. (via Barry Charles Wheeler)

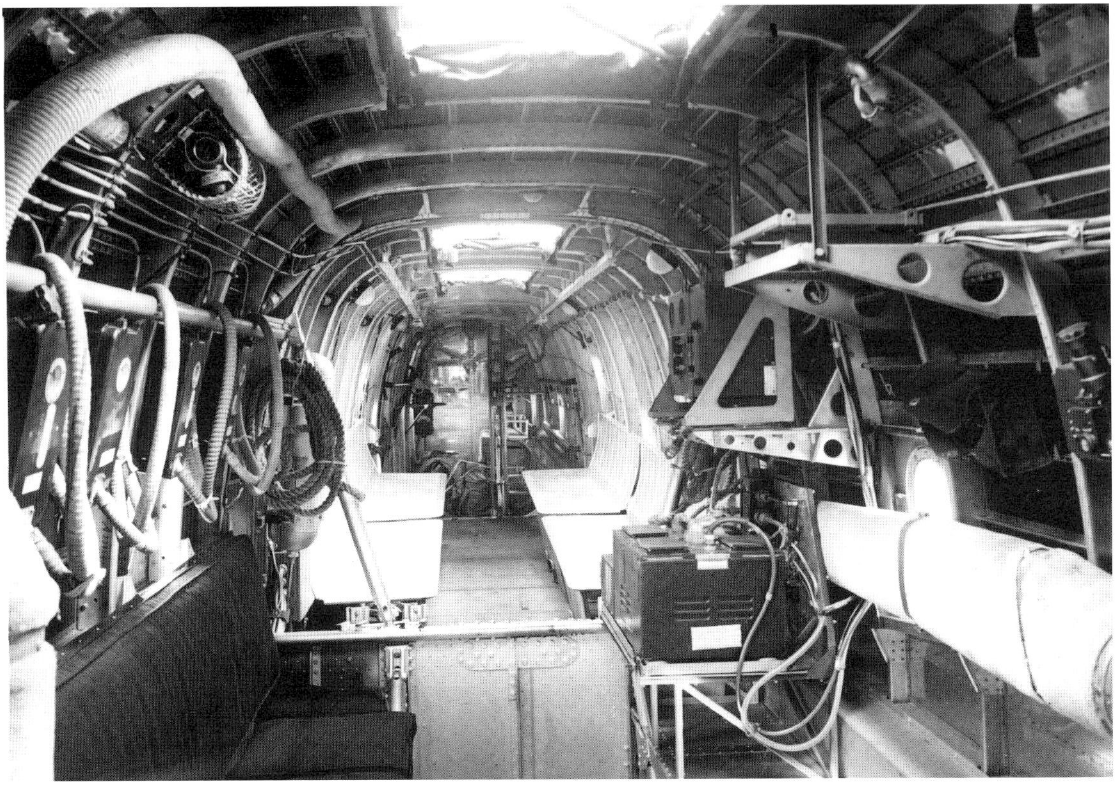

Interior of a new-build A.IX looking aft with paratroop seats in the rear fuselage. (*Aeroplane*)

At a display in 1947, No 295 Sqn showed this A.IX (RT903), a new type for this airborne support unit. It lasted only a year in RAF service before being withdrawn and sold to Aviation Traders. (via Barry Charles Wheeler)

Delivered early in 1946, this rather fine view of A.IX RT796 shows the Halifax in its twilight guise – no guns, bomber camouflage, windows along the side and top of the fuselage. It served first with No 47 Sqn, before transferring to 295 Sqn in September 1947. (via Barry Charles Wheeler)

to 59,000lb, contributed in no small measure to the total collapse of the undercarriage and the aircraft was written off. It was replaced by converted G-AIAR in March.

Other tanker conversions included G-AHDL (w/o with u/c collapse in April), 'HDM, 'HDV, and 'JNW, all flown by Westminster Airways. By the time the three aircraft were withdrawn from tanker flights in July '49, they had flown 368 tanker sorties.

Two Haltons were lost in fatal accidents during the Airlift. Lancashire Aircraft Corp's G-AJZZ crashed near Schleswigland on March 21, 1949, when it struck high ground during an instrument let-down, only the radio officer surviving from the crew of four. On April 30, Halton G-AKAC of World Air Freight crashed west of Oranienburg in the Soviet Zone during a return flight from Tegel; Capt Lewis and his three crew were killed.

Non-fatal accidents involved G-AITC of World Air Freight seriously damaged at Fuhlsbuttel on June 10; Lancashire's Halton G-ALBZ suffered a burst tyre landing at Tegel on June 12; the same company's G-AKFH was written off on June 26 landing at Gatow. The final Lancashire casualty was Halton tanker G-AHWN where the inherent weakness of the undercarriage was demonstrated yet again when it collapsed on landing at Schleswigland on July 6.

The final civil airlift flight on Operation *Plainfare* was flown on August 15, 1949, by Halton G-AIAP piloted by Capt Villa of Eagle Aviation. It carried 14,400lb of flour, landing at Tegel at 01.45hr on August 16. In just over a year, the civil fleet flew 21,921 sorties to Berlin and carried in 146,980 tons of fluids and freight.

After the end of the Berlin Airlift, most of the Halifax/Halton fleet was grounded as C of As ran out and the operators either closed or switched to more efficient types. Parked at airfields around Britain, principally Squires Gate, Southend and Bovingdon, they gradually sagged on their ever-troublesome main legs and almost all went to the breakers.

In August 1946, No 620 Sqn at Aqir, Palestine, was in its last month of operations before being renumbered 113 Sqn. RT879 later served with No 1 Ferry Unit in the Middle East before being sold to Aviation Traders where it became G-ALSL in March 1950. (via Barry Charles Wheeler)

Survivors included G-AITC of World Air Freight which crash-landed at Brindisi on January 20, 1950, and was scrapped. Another was G-AKEC which was entered for the Daily Express Air Race in September 1950. Flown by Capt AN Marshall, it flew round the South Coast of England to come 24th at an average speed of 267mph. By the end of 1953, the Halifax had left the UK air scene.

Halifax – UK Airline Users

Air Freight: Formed in 1946 and registered as a freight operator in February '47. Flew two Halifax VIIIs on flights from Bovingdon and occasionally inbound to Gatwick and Luton, to collect fresh fruit from southern Europe and North Africa. Bought by Harold Bamberg of Eagle Aviation in '48.

Fleet: G-AJBL and 'JBK. G-AKJI and 'KJJ never entered service.

Bond Air Services: Formed at Gatwick by DE Bond in 1946 for general charter work. Halifaxes bought '47 to fly soft fruit from Italy, Spain and southern France. Joined Berlin Airlift operations in August '48 and acquired Haltons and Halifax IXs. After the airlift in '48, retained Halifax/Haltons for further work, but finally withdrawn in May '50 with Bond closing at end of '51.

Fleet: Mk VIII G-AIOH, 'IOI, 'IWW, 'IZO. Mk IX G-ALON, 'LOS. Halton G-AHDN, 'HDO, 'HDP, 'HDS, 'HDT, 'HDW, 'HDX, 'RDU.

British American Air Services: Established 1935 and post-war, in '47, bought Halifax C.VIIIs for charter work and moved from White Waltham to Bovingdon. Took part in Berlin Airlift with aircraft converted to fuel tankers. By early '50, one Halifax remained and the airline closed in August.

Fleet: Mk VIII G-AIAR, 'JPJ, 'KAD, 'KBB, 'KGN. Halton G-AGZP.

Eagle Aviation: Established by Harold Bamberg in April 1948 with Halifax C.VIIIs freighters arriving shortly afterwards. Berlin Airlift from August 26, 1948, with three aircraft. Resumed commercial flights a year later and bought Air Freight, enlarging the Halifax fleet. Avro Yorks acquired and last Halifax lost in non-fatal accident in November '50.

Fleet: G-AIAP, 'IAR, 'JBL, 'JCG, 'KBR, 'LEF.

Chartair: Founded at Thame airfield in August 1946 and established Airtech to overhaul/maintain Halifax aircraft. For Berlin Airlift, installed Rebecca nav aid in 24 Halifaxes and also designed large freight panniers for the type. Chartair merged with British American Air Service in May '47 and in '61 Airtech absorbed the assets of Chartair which finally disappeared.

Fleet: Mk VIII G-AJPJ, 'IAR, 'KGN.

Lancashire Aircraft Corporation (LAC): From a company established in World War Two to repair damaged Bristol Beaufighters, LAC turned to charter flying in 1946 and in September acquired a large

His Highness the Maharajah Gaekwar of Baroda purchased PP336 c/n1398 and in February 1946 it was converted to become the prototype Halton 2 as G-AGZP. Flown on behalf of its owner by British American Air Services it was used for commuting between India and England before being sold to Alpha Airways in April 1947. (via *Aeroplane*)

A veteran of the Berlin Airlift, Halifax C.VIII G-AITC (PP320) joined World Air Freight at Bovingdon in April 1949 and flew 264 cargo sorties into the beleaguered city. Undercarriage failure at Brindisi in 1950 brought about its demise. (via Barry Charles Wheeler)

number of Halifaxes. In April '47, G-AIHV was first conversion for civil use. Fleet undertook world-wide flights, including first by UK civil type ('IHY) to Budapest December 11, 1947. LAC heavily involved in Berlin Airlift, its 12 aircraft flying 2,760 sorties, more than any other charter company, over 2,500 by freighters converted into tankers.

By October '49, LAC had four Halifaxes in service with seven tankers in reserve. They flew charters carrying diverse cargoes such as fruit, textiles and penicillin, as well as 50 tons of beer from Tadcaster to Antwerp in September '50. By mid-1952, the company retained one Halifax, but Avro Yorks were now LAC's main type.

Fleet: Mk VI total of 22 never entered service; Mk VIII G-AHWN, 'HYH, 'HYI, 'IHU-HY, 'ILO, 'JZY-ZZ, 'KBJ, 'KBK, 'KEC, 'KXT, 'LBS-BV, 'LBZ, 'LCX; Halton 'GZP, 'HDV.

London Aero & Motor Services (LAMS): Established in early-1946 by West End car hire group, Grosvenor Square Garages under Dr Graham Humby. Halifaxes acquired and company name changed to LAMS. Based at Elstree, but smallness of airfield saw move to Stansted December '46. Aircraft flew soft fruits from southern Europe to UK and various charters tramping around world. One aircraft based in Australia. Humby succumbed to tuberculosis and company wound down, closing in July '48.

Fleet: Mk VI seven acquired but never entered service; Mk VIII G-AHZJ-ZO, 'IWI-WP, 'IWR, 'IWT, 'JPK, 'KBR, 'KJF; Halton ZS-BTA.

Payloads: Associate of London Aero and Motor Services, Payloads was formed in late 1946. Acquired Halifaxes for conversion to freighters, but used few, most going to LAMS. Payload closed following collapse of LAMS, Halifaxes going to other users.

Fleet: Mk VIII G-AIWN, 'IWT; G-AJNT-NZ and 'JPK never entered service.

Skyflight: Established August 1948 with start of Berlin Airlift and flew three Halifax VIIIs from Wunsdorf. Switched to other freight flights before ceasing operations in May '49.

Fleet: Mk VIII G-AHZK, 'HZO, 'IWI, 'IWP, 'KBR. G-AHYI & 'IID never entered service.

Westminster Airways: Formed June 1946 by Members of Parliament. Bought Haltons for Berlin Airlift, beginning freighter sorties from Hamburg December '48 and with tankers flying in diesel oil in January '49 until July when fleet withdrawn. Brief period servicing aircraft at Blackbushe Airport, but company closed October '51.

Fleet: Haltons G-AHDL, 'HDM, 'HDV. Mk VIII G-AJNW.

Worldair Carriers: Began freight flights from Bovingdon February 1950. Fatal accident to Halton G-AHDX in Alps in April killed two Worldair directors, effectively closing the company.

World Air Freight: Formed June 1947 and cargo flights with first of four Halifax VIIIs began from Stansted in November. Moved to Bovingdon February '48. Joined Berlin Airlift October '48, but aircraft crashed at Gatow. Replaced in November, but this lost April '49 with crew. Single Halifax continued until withdrawn August '49. Company ceased trading after sole aircraft damaged at Brindisi January '50.

Fleet: G-AITC, 'JNZ, 'KAC, 'KGZ.

BOAC HP.70 Halton Fleet				
Reg	*c/n*	*Serial*	*CofA*	*Remarks*
G-AHDL	1308	PP224	18.9.46	*Fitzroy*. To Westminster AW; cr Gatow 1.4.49
G-AHDM	1312	PP228	20.7.46	*Falmouth*. To Westminster AW; b/u Blackbushe 9.50
G-AHDN	1318	PP234	24.3.47	*Flamborough*. To Bond AS; b/u Southend 11.50
G-AHDO	1320	PP236	13.8.47	*Forfar*. To Bond AS; b/u Southend 11.50
G-AHDP	1341	PP268	24.3.47	*Fleetwood*. To Bond AS; w/o Germany 9.4.49
G-AHDR	1342	PP269	7.7.47	*Foreland*. To Louis Breguet as F-BECK 6.48
G-AHDS	1350	PP277	24.8.46	*Freemantle*. To Bond AS; destroyed 27.3.51
G-AHDT	1370	PP308	4.6.47	*Fife*. To Bond AS; scrapped Germany 11.49
G-AHDU	1372	PP310	10.7.46	*Falkirk*. To Bond AS; b/u Southend 11.50
G-AHDV	1376	PP314	19.8.46	*Finisterre*. To Westminster AW; dbr Squires Gate 17.10.52
G-AHDW	1377	PP315	29.7.46	*Falaise*. To Bond AS; b/u Southend 11.50
G-AHDX	1378	PP316	4.6.47	*Folkestone*. To Bond AS; cr in Alps 16.4.50
Handley Page HP.70 Halton 2				
G-AGZP	1398	PP336	20.3.46	Maharajah Gaekwar of Baroda; to ZS-BTA; Lanc AC; b/u Bovingdon 3.53

Westminster Airways took delivery of G-AJNW in April 1949 and undertook 116 tanker airlift flights to Berlin before its C of A expired exactly a year later. In December 1950 it became a film star when it took the part of the Reindeer aircraft in *No Highway*, for which it was fitted with a tricycle undercarriage, four 'jets' and a single fin and rudder. (via Barry Charles Wheeler)

Named *Air Voyager*, G-AKEC was one of 13 aircraft chartered by the British government in September 1948 for two months to fly 350,000 gallons of milk a week from Belfast to Liverpool and Blackpool airports. Part of the Lancashire Aircraft Corp fleet, the C.VIII also flew in the Berlin Airlift and took part in the Daily Express Air Race in September 1950. (via *Aeroplane*)

Without its pannier, Eagle Aviation's G-ALEF Red Eagle looks uncomfortably strange. It was withdrawn from use at Luton in August 1951. (via *Aeroplane*)

An overseas user of the C.VIII was SANA (Societe Auxiliaire de Navigation Aérienne) which operated four. F-BESE was former PP223 which served with 301 Sqn until sold in June 1948. It succumbed to an engine fire at Blackbushe the following year. (via *Aeroplane*)

Above: Just so much scrap. Halifax A.IX RT816 of the RAF Transport Command Development Unit became G-AMCG following its withdrawal from service but suffered the ignominy of being scrapped at Southend after arriving in May 1950. (via *Aeroplane*)

Below and opposite: Christened *Port of Sydney*, G-AIWT was one of 12 Halifax C.VIIIs bought by LAMS for freight work. Embarking on a round-the-world tramping flight on April 23, 1947, the aircraft was commanded by Capt Thiele, accompanied by LAMS owner, Dr Graham Humby, and seven crew. The aircraft flew a number of charters in Australasia and returned to its Stansted base on June 5, bearing seven tons of dripping from the people of New South Wales as a gift for the victims of winter floods in England. Humby is seen on the right in the picture with NSW Agent-General, Hon John Tully. (via Barry Charles Wheeler/Philip Jarrett)

LAMS
PORT OF SYDNEY
New South Wales

BOAC's first Handley Page Halton G-AHDU was christened *Falkirk* by Lady Winster, wife of Lord Winster, Minister of Civil Aviation, at Radlett on July 18, 1946. The BOAC crew and Sir Frederick Handley Page (fourth from right) at the naming ceremony under the nose of the first Halton.

The aircraft, seen in the colour photograph, began proving flights in August under the command of Capt W Buchanan, its cruising speed of 220mph and relatively low noise levels in the passenger cabin were considered an advance over other types. (via *Aeroplane*/Philip Jarrett)

Chapter 15

Halifax Production

In addition to the main Handley Page factories at Radlett and Cricklewood, the Halifax was the subject of a major Ministry of Aircraft Production plan to build the bomber under contract by a number of companies around Britain. A Halifax Group was set up to control these dispersed companies of which English Electric at Preston was the largest, having previously built Hampdens.

The others were Fairey Aviation at Stockport, Rootes Securities at Liverpool Speke, and five component manufacturers that made up the London Aircraft Production Group with headquarters at Leavesden. Between them and including the two prototypes they built a total of 6,178 Halifaxes of all marks over a seven-year period. This was nearly 4,000 more than the Stirling (2,375) and only nearly 1,200 less than the Lancaster (7,374).

The individual production figures were:

English Electric	2,145
Handley Page	1,592
Fairey Aviation	1,070
London Aircraft Production Group	710
Rootes Securities	661

RAF ground crew trainees were seconded to Halifax production centres to gain experience on the aircraft prior to posting to a front-line squadron or a heavy conversion unit. This is a Rootes-built B.V Srs 1 (Special) and while some find out about the intricacies of the Merlin XX engine, others inspect the main undercarriage, and with the help of a cart, the mysteries of the multi-door bomb-bay. (via *Aeroplane*)

Production Batches

Aircraft were delivered between October 1940 and the final batch received between September and November 1946. Note that some blocks have numbers deleted for security purposes.

L7244-L7245 HP.56/57 Halifax prototypes built to Spec P.13/36. F/f 25.10.39

L9485-L9534, L9560-L9584, L9600-L9608 (84) Mk.I.

L9609-L9624 (16) Mk.II.

R9363-R9540 (100) Mk.II, R9534 was Mk.III prototype.

V9976-V9994, W1002-W1276 (200) Mk.II built by English Electric.

W7650-W7939 (200) Mk.II.

BB189-BB446 (200) Mk.II built by LAP.

DG219-DG230 (12) Mk.II, DG231-DG253, DG270-DG317, DG338-DG363, DG384-DG424 (138) Mk.V Built by Rootes.

DJ980-DK271 (150) Mk.V built by Fairey Aviation.

DT481-DT808 (250) Mk.II built by English Electric.

DZ779-EA201 (250) cancelled order.

EB127-EB276 (100) Mk.V built by Rootes.

HR654-HR988 (250) Mk.II, HR909 fitted with trial turrets.

HX147-HX191, HX222-HX225 Mk.II; HX226-HX247, HX265-HX296, HX311-HX357 (150) Mk.III.

JB781-JD476 (350) Mk.II built by English Electric. JD212 trialled RPs, JD300 fitted with ventral 0.5in gun.

JN882-JP338 (250) Mk.II built by LAP.

LK626-LK667, LK680-LK711, LK725-LK746 Mk.V; LK747-LK766, LK779-LK812, LK826-LK850, LK863-LK887 (200) Mk.III built by Fairey Aviation.

LK890-LK932, LK945-LK976, LK988-LK999, LL112-LL153, LL167-LL198, LL213-LL258, LL270-LL312, LL325-LL367, LL380-LL423, LL437-LL469, LL481-LL521, LL534-LL542 Mk.V; LL543-LL559, LL573-LL615 (480) Mk.III built by Rootes.

LV771-LV799, LV813-LV842, LV857-LV883, LV898-LV923, LV935-LV973, LV985-LV999, LW113-LW143, LW157-LW179, LW191-LW195 B.III; LW196-LW210 (240) B.VII.

LW223-LW246, LW259-LW301, LW313-LW345 (100) B.II.

LW346-LW348, LW361-LW397, LW412-LW446, LW459-LW481, LW495-LW522, LW537-LW559, LW572LW598, LW613-LW658, LW671-LW696, LW713-LW724 (260) B.III built by English Electric.

MZ282-MZ495 (180) B.III built by LAP.

MZ500-MZ939 (360) B.III built by English Electric.

MZ495-NA309 B.III; NA310-NA468 (340) A.VII. NA469-NA488 cancelled. Built by Rootes.

NA492-NA704 (180) B.III built by Fairey.

NP681-NP820 B.VII; NP715, NP752, NP753 B.VI; NP821-NP927 (200) B.VI.

NP930-NR290 (200) B.III built by English Electric.

PN167-PN207 B.III; PN208, PN223-PN242 B.VII; PN243-PN267, PN285-PN327, PN343, A.VII (131) built by Fairey.

PN365-PN406, PN423-PN460 (80) B.III built by LAP.

PP142-PP164 renumbered TW774-TW796, PP165-PP187, PP203-PP216 B.VI; PP217-PP243 C.VIII; PP244-PP247 A.VIII; PP259-PP296, PP308-PP338 C.VIII; PP339-PP350, PP362-PP389 A.VII (200).

RG345-RG390, RG413-RG446 (80) B.III; RG447-RG458, RG472-RG479 (20) B.VII; RG480-RG879 (300) B.VI built by English Electric.

RS227-RS497 (200) cancelled order for Fairey.

RT753-RT757 (5) A.VII; RT758-RT938 (145) A.IX; further 50 cancelled.

RV104-RV290 (150) cancelled order for LAP.
ST794-ST818 (25) B/GR.VI built by English Electric. Further 350 cancelled.
SV344-SV736 cancelled order for A.VII from Rootes.
TH186-TH446 (200) B.VI cancelled order.
TM944-TN247 (150) cancelled order with Fairey.
VG768-VG908 (110) A.IX cancelled order

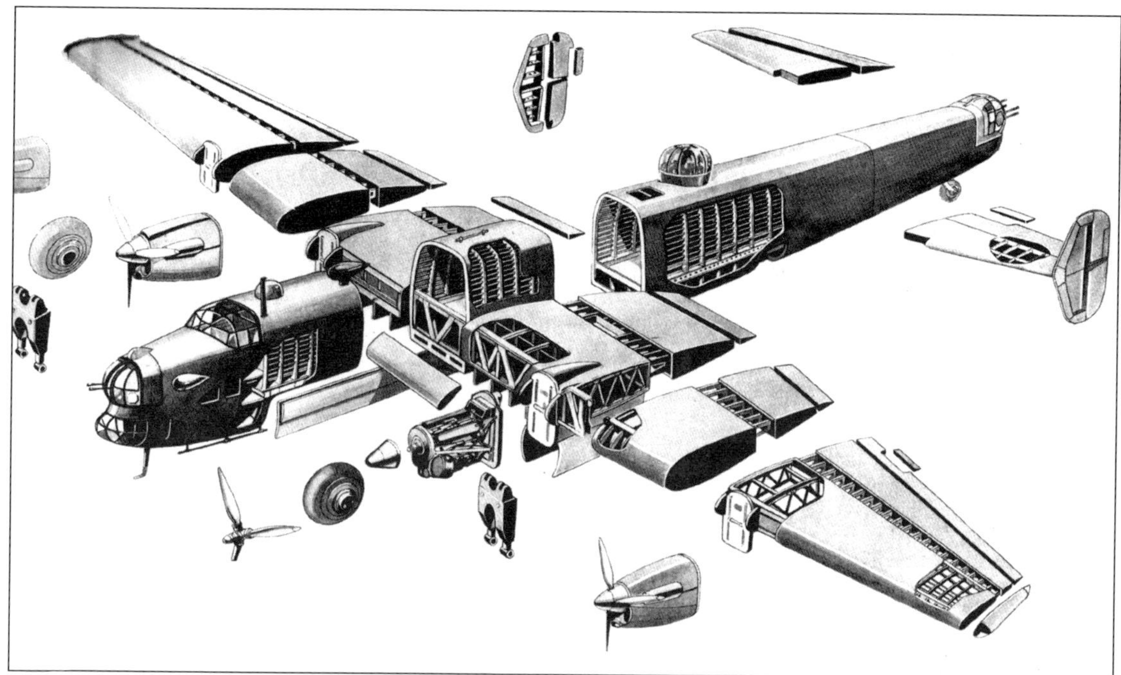

Above: Exploded view showing the break-down of parts for ease of manufacture.

Right: At a main production centre, believed to be the Handley Page factory at Cricklewood, heavy presses stamp out airframe parts. (Aeroplane)

Halifaxes on the British Civil Register

B.III: G-AGXA ex-NR169. Reg: 16.5.46 sold in Australia 7.47 as VH-BDT; G-AJPG ex-NA684. Instructional airframe, scrapped at Cranfield 12.48

B.VI: G-AIBG ex-RG790. B/u Stansted 1948; G-AJBE ex-RG785. To Pakistan AF 10.49; G-AJSZ ex-RG722. B/u Bovingdon 1948; G-AJTX to 'JUB (5) ex-RG720, '756, '757, '824, '825. B/u Bovingdon 1948; G-AKAP ex-RG763. Reg OO-XAB but b/u Thame .48; G-AKAW ex-RG784. To Pakistan AF 10.49; G-AKBI ex-RG716. B/u Bovingdon 5.48; G-AKJI-JJ ex-RG695/RG698. B/u Doncaster 1948; G-AKLI-LJ-LK ex-RG783-RG781-RG779. To Pakistan AF 10.49; G-AKNG-NL ex-RG658-RG700-RG717-RG759-RG712-PP171. B/u at Bovingdon 5.48; G-AKUT-UU ex-RG736-RG813. To Pakistan AF 10.49/B/u 7.50; G-ALCD ex-ST808. B/u Bovingdon .49; G-ALCY-CZ ex-RG719-RG774. B/u Bovingdon 5.48; G-ALDZ-LEE ex-RG822-RG826-RG827-RG847-RG853-RG877. B/u Bovingdon 5.49; G-ALOM ex-ST801. B/u Southend 11.49

C.VIII: G-AGPC ex-PP287 to France as F-BCJS 10.47; G-AGTK ex-PP274 to France as F-BCJX 8.47; G-AHKK ex-PP309 to France as F-BCJV 7.47; G-AHVT ex-PP278 to France as F-BCJR 9.47; G-AHWL-WN ex-PP331-PP238-PP230 to France as F-BCJT 10.47/To 'JZY 6.47/B/u Bovingdon 8.50; G-AHYH-YI ex-PP261-PP311 b/u Woolsington 10.49/B/u Bovingdon .49; G-AHZJ ex-PP247 crashed Bergamo, Italy, 7.47; G-AHZK ex-PP246 b/u Stansted .50; G-AHZL ex-PP242 b/u Stansted 6.49; G-AHZM ex-PP260 u/c collapsed Elstree 9.46, later b/u; G-AHZN ex-PP244 ditched off Le Zoute, Belgium 9.46; G-AHZO ex-PP239 b/u Stansted 6.49; G-AIAN-AO ex-PP271-PP272 restored to RAF and cancelled 4.47; G-AIAP ex-PP281 crashed Calcutta, India, 11.50; dbr; G-AIAR ex-PP326 wfu at Thame 10.50; G-AIAS ex-PP327 dbr Aldermaston 11.46; b/u 4.49; G-AIHU ex-PP222 crashed in Males 5.12.47; G-AIHV ex-PP262 b/u Stansted .52; G-AIHW ex-PP284 crashed Heathrow 5.6.47; G-AIHX ex-PP294 crashed Squires Gate 3.9.48; G-AIHY ex-PP241 dbr Le Bourget, France, 28.12.49; G-AIID ex-PP317 b/u Bovingdon 20.3.50; G-AILO ex-PP280 b/u Bovingdon 8.51; G-AIOH ex-PP240 crashed Barcelona 30.5.47; G-AIOI ex-

The centre-section of a Halifax B.II incorporating the inner engine nacelles with the main undercarriage doors already attached.

PP243 dbr Tegel, Berlin, 15.2.49; G-AITC ex-PP320 dbr Brindisi, Italy 20.1.50; G-AIWI ex-PP218 b/u Bovingdon 5.49; G-AIWJ ex-PP286 wfu Stansted .49; to Fire School; b/u 10.51; G-AIWK ex-PP295 vandalised Mascot, Aust; b/u .48; G-AIWL ex-PP291 to Stansted Fire School; b/u .51; G-AIWM ex-PP266 to Stansted Fire School; b/u Cardiff FS; G-AIWN ex-PP235 wfu Southend 5.50; G-AIWO ex-PP290 for spares at Stansted; G-AIWP ex-PP299 b/u Stansted 3.50; G-AIWR ex-PP245 to ZS-BUL 12.47; G-AIWT ex-PP265 dbr Bovingdon 9.47; G-AIZO ex-PP293 crash-landed Studham 23.5.48; G-AJBK ex-PP264 to F-BCJZ 10.47; G-AJBL ex-PP276 b/u Bovingdon .49; G-AJCG ex-PP328 reg LN-OAS, b/u Lydda .49; G-AJNT ex-PP259 to F-BCQX 6.47; G-AJNU ex-PP279 to AP-ACH 5.48; G-AJNV ex-PP292 to HB-AIF 8.47; G-AJNW ex-PP296 wfu Blackbushe 4.50; G-AJNX ex-PP312 to AP-ABZ 5.48; G-AJNY ex-PP322 to AP-ACG 5.48; G-AJNZ ex-PP323 crashed Isle of Man 21.10.48; G-AJPJ ex-PP263 to Israel, crashed Lydda, 20.7.48; G-AJPK ex-PP313 b/u Thame .50; G-AJXD ex-PP330 to F-BCJQ 6.47; G-AJZY ex-PP238 crashed Gt Missenden 8.3.51; G-AJZZ ex-PP334 crashed Schleswigland, Germany 21.3.49; G-AKAD ex-PP283 dbr Rennes, France 17.5.48; G-AKBA ex-PP219 crashed Albacete, Spain 25.5.48; G-AKBB ex-PP237 dbr at Schleswigland, Germany 11.2.49; G-AKBJ ex-PP233 dbr Tegel, Berlin 1.6.49; G-AKBK ex-PP231 wfu Bovingdon 8.50; G-AKBP ex-PP289 to HB-AIL 9.47; G-AKBR ex-PP329 ex-G-AKIE & HB-AIM, b/u Germany .50; G-AKCT ex-PP273 ex HB-AIK, to Egypt AF 12.48; G-AKEC ex-PP282 dbr by Halton 'HDV at Squires Gate 17.12.52; G-AKGN ex-PP333 scrapped Thame 4.50; G-AKGO ex-PP324 to Stansted Fire School & Cardiff .52; G-AKGP ex-PP223 to F-BESE 6.48; G-AKGZ ex-PP338 crashed Gatow, Germany 8.10.48; G-AKJF ex-PP217 to Stansted Fire School 5.52; G-AKXT ex-PP220 wfu Bovingdon 12.49; G-ALBS-LBV ex-229, 270, 319, 321, all scrapped Bovingdon 8.50; G-ALBZ ex-PP275 collided with 'HWN at Schleswigland 10.5.49; G-ALCX ex-PP335 wfu Bovingdon 11.49, scrapped .52; G-ALEF ex-PP337 ex-LN-OAT wfu Luton 11.50

A.IX: G-AKKP ex-RT885 used for spares .11.50; G-AKKU ex-RT892 used for spares .11.50; G-ALIR ex-RT791 used for spares, b/u Southend 11.50; G-ALON ex-RT763 wfu Southend 6.50; G-ALOO ex-RT787 to Egypt AF as 1158 2.50; G-ALOP ex-RT846 to Egypt AF as 1155 12.49; G-ALOR ex-RT888 to Egypt AF as 1157 2.50; G-ALOS ex-RT937 wfu Southend 6.50; G-ALSK ex-RT832 scrapped Southend 12.51; G-ALSL ex-RT879 b/u Hawarden 11.50; G-ALUT, LUU, LUV ex-RT924, 848, 873 scrapped Southend 11.50; G-ALVH ex-RT788 to Egypt AF as 1163 5.50; G-ALVI ex-RT793 to Egypt AF as 1156 1.50; G-ALVJ ex-RT852 to Egypt AF as 1159 2.50; G-ALVK ex-RT901 to Egypt AF as 1160 3.50; G-ALVL ex-RT907 to Egypt AF as 1162 4.50; G-ALVM ex-RT938 to Egypt AF as 1161 3.50; G-ALYI, YJ, YK, YL, YM, YN ex-RT884, 776, 785, 837, 772, 762 scrapped Southend 1950; G-AMBX ex-RT759 scrapped Hawarden 2.51; G-AMCB, CC, CD, CE, CF, CG ex-RT 895, 836, 893, 890, 935, 816 used for spares at Southend .50.

Assembly underway with the Boulton-Paul mid-upper turret installed and the rear fuselage joined to the mid-section.

In another part of the factory, Rolls-Royce Merlins are located into their bearers and final adjustments made.

Two assembly lines of Halifax B.IIs head towards completion and air test, probably at Radlett. The aircraft on the left-hand side awaits its outer wing sections.

Above left: A centre-fuselage with a cut-out in the roof structure for the mid-upper turret.

Above right: A newly completed bomb-bay with the carriers in position and doors fitted.

A production line of B.III noses, much refined from the earlier turreted versions.

Above: The business end of a line of Halifax B.II noses, their B-P turrets and bomb-aimers windows installed and workers putting the last pieces on each section.

Above: Women formed increasingly a major part of Britain's workforce as the war progressed and available men were called up for military service. After training, women performed almost every task in aircraft assembly, working in factories that turned out small training types as well as those producing four-engine bombers.

Right: Typical of the drawings found in Halifax manuals is this November 1941 illustration of the bomb compartment located between fuselage frames 8 and 29

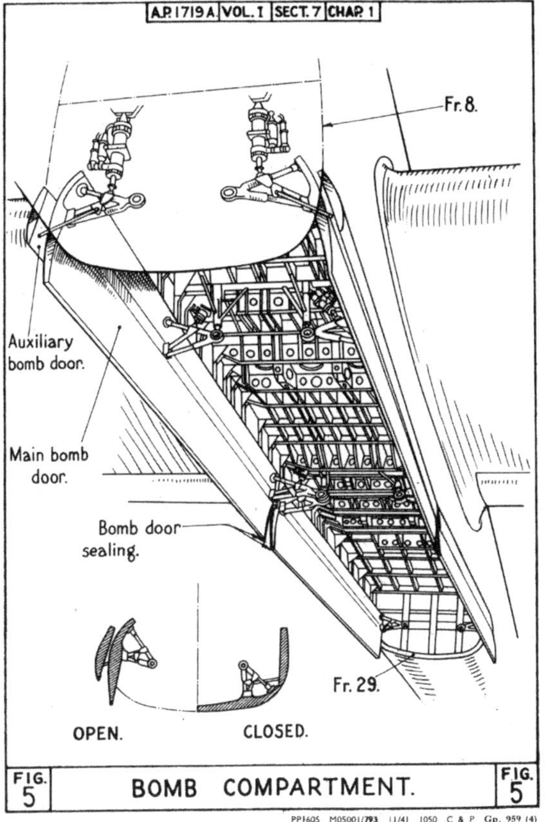

Wing and tail sections for a B.III, still in their metal finish before going to the paint shop for camouflaging.

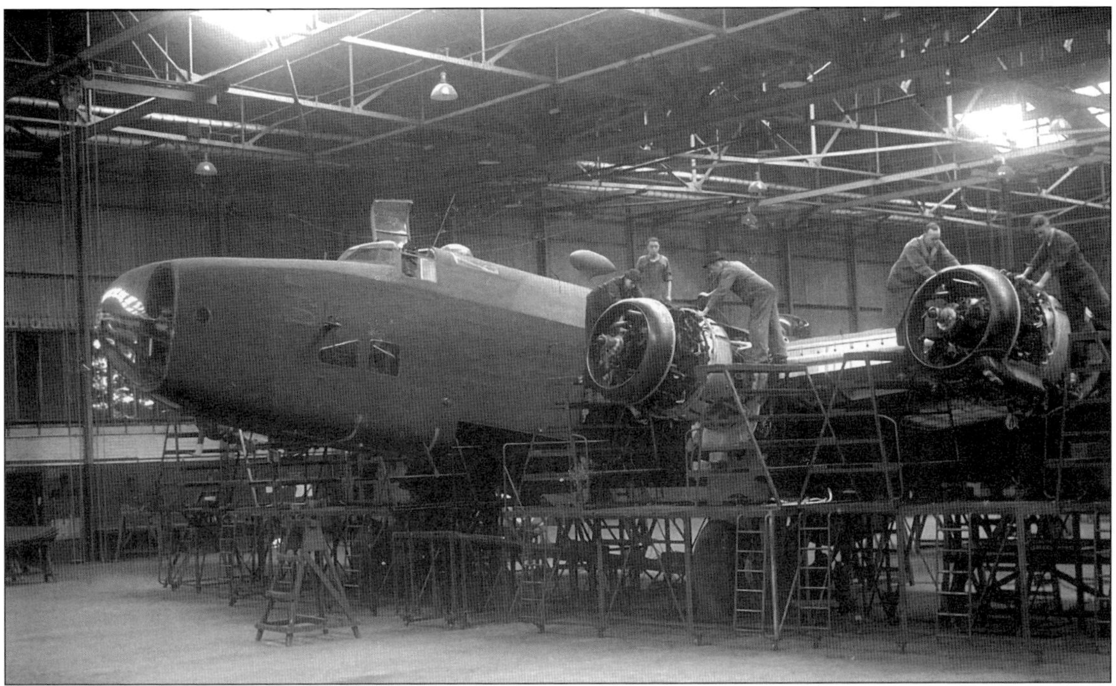

Bristol Hercules radial engines are attached to a B.III.

An official diagram showing the main structure of a Halifax B.III.

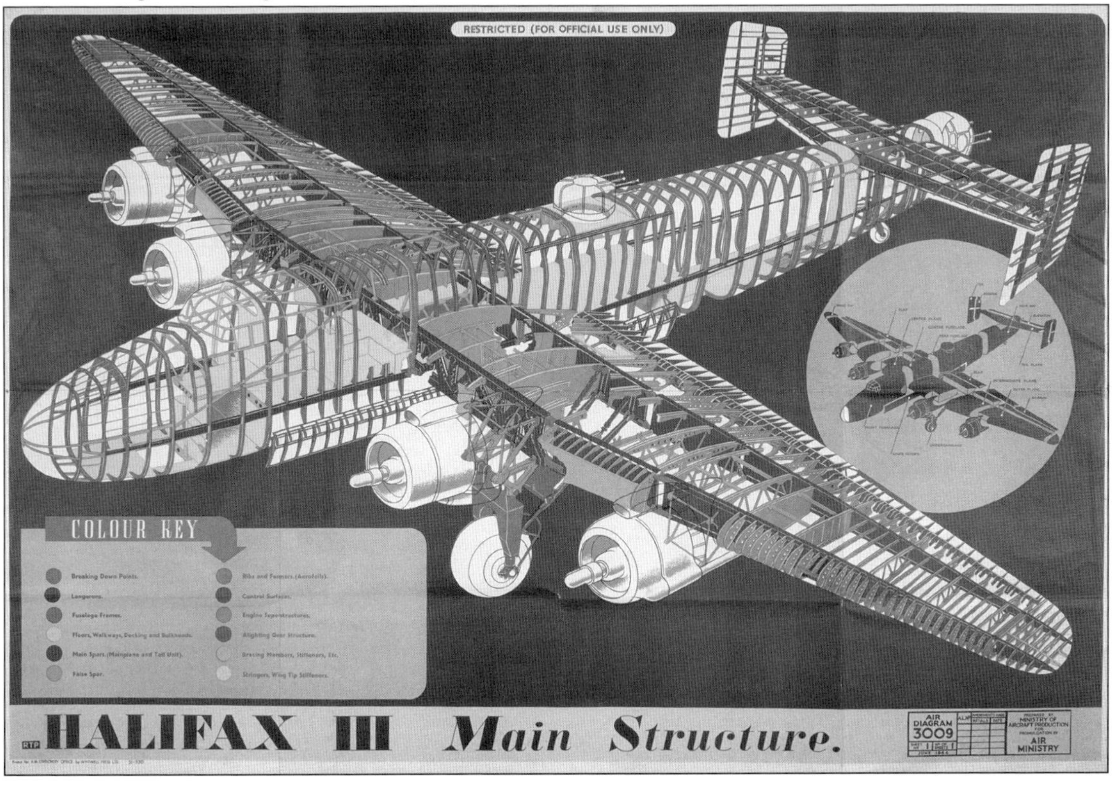

Chapter 16

The Halifax in Service

The following is a comprehensive listing of RAF, Commonwealth and foreign operators and squadrons which flew the Handley Page Halifax from 1941 until withdrawal from service.

Royal Air Force Bomber Command

10 Squadron

Motto: *Rem acu tangere* (To hit the mark). Formed January 1, 1915. Received Halifax B.IIs December 1941 based at Leeming, Yorks. Detachment to Middle East, June '42. Sqn moved to Melbourne, Yorks, Aug '42. Halifax B.IIIs from March '44 to May '45.

35 Squadron

Motto: *Uno animo agimus* (We act with one accord). Formed February 1, 1916. Received Halifax B.Is November 1940 based at Leeming, Yorks, later to Linton-on Ouse and Graveley, Hunts. First Halifax sorties March 11/12, 1941. Halifax B.IIs and B.IIIs to March '44 when converted to Lancaster B.I/IIIs. First squadron loss was B.I L9499 TL-Q shot down returning from Kiel on June 30, 1941. B.II W1048 recovered from Norwegian lake in 1973 and now in the RAF Museum.

51 Squadron

Motto: *Swift and sure.* Formed May 15, 1916. Received Halifax B.IIs November '42 based at Snaith, Yorks; B.IIIs from January '44.

76 Squadron

Motto: *Resolute.* Formed Sept 15, 1916. Received Halifax B.Is and B.IIs from May '41 based at Linton-on-Ouse. Moved to Middleton St George, Co Durham, June '41 before moving back to Linton in Sept '42 and Holme-on-Spalding Moor, Yorks from June '43. Halifax B.Vs from Apr '43, B.IIIs from Feb '44, B.VIs from Mar '45 to May '45. Sustained first RAF Halifax lost to enemy action – B.I L9492 shot down

Sirius was a B.VI operated by the Empire Air Navigation School formed at Shawbury in October 1944. Coded FGF-B, ST814 was one of a number of Halifaxes on strength. Note the scanner visible in the transparent H2S blister. (via Barry Charles Wheeler)

over Kiel by Oblt Reinhold Eckardt, II/NJG1, on June 24, 1941. B.I L9530 MP-L shot down on Berlin raid on Aug 12/13, 1941, with pilot, Flt Lt C Cheshire, brother of Leonard Cheshire VC, made PoW; two of the seven crew killed.

77 Squadron
Motto: *Esse potius quam videri* (To be, rather than seem). Formed October 1, 1916. Received Halifax B.IIs from October 1942 based at Elvington, Yorks; B.Vs from late '43, B.IIIs from May '44, B.VIs in Mar–May '45.

78 Squadron
Motto: *Nemo non Paratus* (Nobody unprepared). Formed November 1, 1916. Received Halifax B.IIs from March '42 at Croft, Co Durham. To Middleton St George, Co Durham, June '42, later to Linton and Breighton, Yorks. B.IIIs from January '44, B.VIs from April '45.

102 (Ceylon) Squadron
Motto: *Tentate et perficite* (Attempt and achieve). Formed August 1917. Received Halifax B.IIs from Dec '41 based at Dalton, Yorks, to Topcliffe and Pocklington until May '45. B.IIIs arrived from May '44 and B.VIs between Feb and May '45.

First squadron loss on operations was B.II W1099 which crashed on return to Cottesmore, but without casualties.

103 Squadron
Motto: *Noli me tangere* (Touch me not). Formed September 1, 1917. Received Halifax B.IIs from July '42 based at Elsham Wolds, Lincs, but became Lancaster-equipped from Oct '42.

158 Squadron
Motto: *Strength in unity.* Formed September 1918. Received Halifax B.IIs June '42 based at East Moor, Yorks, later to Rufforth (Nov '42) and Lissett (Feb '43). B.IIIs from Dec '43 to May '45 and B.VIs from Apr '45.

Operated two famous long-serving B.IIIs, LV907 NP-F *Friday the 13th* which logged 128 missions, and LV917 NP-C *Clueless* with 99.

171 Squadron
Motto: *Per dolum defendimus* (We defend by confusion). Formed at Gatwick June 15, 1942. Switched from fighters to radio-countermeasures in Sept '44, taking Stirlings first then Halifax B.IIIs from Oct. Based at North Creake, Norfolk, and disbanded July '45.

178 Squadron
Motto: *Irae emissarii* (Emissaries of wrath). Formed January 15, 1943. Received Halifax B.IIs briefly from May '43 to Sep '43 to supplement Liberators based in Libya for ME ops.

192 Squadron
Motto: *Dare to discover.* Formed at Gainsborough September 5, 1917. In bomber support and jamming roles with Halifax B.IIs at Gransden Lodge Jan '43, Mk Vs at Feltwell in July '43 and Mk IIIs from Feb '44 at Foulsham until disbandment Aug '45.

199 Squadron
Motto: *Let tyrants tremble.* Formed November 1917. Received Halifax B.IIIs for bomber support ops from Feb to July '45 based at North Creake, Norfolk. Used on radio counter-measures duties

with Stirlings within 100 Group. Halifaxes frequently combined Window and Mandrel patrols with bombing ops.

346 (Guyenne) Squadron French Air Force

No motto.Formed at Elvington, Yorks, May 16, 1944, with Halifax B.Vs and began operations June 1, 1944. B.IIIs from June '44 and B.VIs between March and Oct '45. Squadron ceased to be RAF controlled in Oct '45, returning to France with a number of Halifaxes.

347 (Tunisie) Squadron French Air Force

No motto. Formed at Elvington, Yorks, June 20, 1944, with Halifax B.Vs and began operations June 27/28, 1944. B.IIIs arrived from July '44 and B.VIs between March and Oct '45. Squadron ceased to be RAF controlled in Oct '45, returning to France with a number of Halifaxes.

405 (Vancouver) Squadron, RCAF

Motto: *Ducimus* (We lead). Formed at Driffield, Yorks, April 23, 1941. First Canadian bomber squadron. Received Halifax B.IIs April '42, based at Topcliffe, Yorks. Moved to Gransden Lodge, Beds, in April '43, Halifaxes replaced by Lancasters Aug '43, becoming part of No 8 (Pathfinder) Group. Flew the well-known B.II W7710 LQ-R *Ruhr Valley Express*.

408 (Goose) Squadron RCAF

Motto: *For freedom.* Formed at Lindholme, Yorks, June 24, 1941. Received Halifax B.Vs Oct '42 based at Leeming, Yorks; B.IIs Dec '42 and Aug '43, then swapped for Lancasters. In July '44 Halifax B.IIIs and VIIs returned until May '45.

415 (Swordfish) Squadron RCAF

Motto: *Ad metam* (To the mark). Formed at Thorney Island, Hants, August 20, 1941. Received Halifax B.IIIs in July '44 based at East Moor, Yorks, with some B.VIIs arriving in '45.

419 (Moose) Squadron RCAF

Motto: *Moosa asmayita* (Moose attacking). Formed at Mildenhall, Suffolk, December 15, 1941. Received Halifax B.IIs in Nov '42 based at Middleton St George, Co Durham. Changed to Lancasters April '44.

420 (Snowy Owl) Squadron RCAF

Motto: *Pugnamus finitum* (We fight to a finish). Formed at Waddington, Lincs, December 19, 1941. Received Halifax B.IIIs from Dec '43 based at Tholthorpe, Yorks.

424 (Tiger) Squadron RCAF

Motto: *Castigandos castigamus* (We chastise those who deserve to be chastised). Formed at Topcliffe, Yorks, October 15, 1942. Received Halifax B.IIIs in Dec '43 based at Skipton-on-Swale, Yorks. Exchanged for Lancasters Jan '45.

425 (Alouette) Squadron RCAF

Motto: *Je te plumerai* (I shall pluck you). French-Canadian unit formed at Dishforth, Yorks, June 22, 1942. Received Halifax B.IIIs Dec '43 at Tholthorpe, Yorks. Retained type to end of war when Lancasters replaced the Halifaxes.

The much-photographed Halifax B.II Srs 1 EY-B of No 78 Sqn is preserved in pictures for all time, but as an aircraft it failed to return from a raid on Mainz on August 12, 1942. (via Barry Charles Wheeler)

426 (Thunderbird) Squadron RCAF

Motto: *On wings of fire*. Formed at Dishforth, Yorks, October 15, 1942. Received Halifax B.IIIs and VIIs from April '44 to May '45 when operating from Linton-on-Ouse, Yorks.

427 (Lion) Squadron RCAF

Motto: *Ferte Manus Certas* (Strike sure). Formed at Croft, Co Durham, November 7, 1942. Received Halifax B.Vs from May '43 at Leeming, Yorks, and IIIs between Jan '44 and Mar '45. Lancasters replaced Halifaxes for last two months of war.

428 (Ghost) Squadron RCAF

Motto: *Usque ad finem* (To the very end). Formed at Dalton, Yorks, November 7, 1942. Received Halifax B.Vs from June '43 based at Middleton St George, Co Durham; B.IIs between Nov '43 and June '44 when re-equipped with Lancasters.

429 (Bison) Squadron RCAF

Motto: *Fortunae nihil* (Nothing to chance). Formed at East Moor, Yorks, November 7, 1942. Received Halifax B.IIs based at Leeming, Yorks, Aug '43, with B.Vs arriving from Nov '43 and B.IIIs from Mar '44. Re-equipped with Lancasters from Mar '45.

431 (Iroquois) Squadron RCAF

Motto: *The hatiten ronteriios* (Warriors of the air). Formed at Burn, Yorks, November 11, 1942. Received Halifax B.Vs from Jul '43 based at Tholthorpe, Yorks; B.IIIs from Mar '44 until Oct '44 when re-equipped with Lancasters.

432 (Leaside) Squadron RCAF

Motto: *Saeviter ad lucem* (Ferociously towards the light). Formed at Skipton-on-Swale, Yorks, May 1, 1943. Received Halifax B.IIIs and VIIs from Feb '44 based at East Moor, Yorks.
  The 12th Canadian squadron formed overseas in World War Two.

433 (Porcupine) Squadron RCAF

Motto: *Quis'y frotte s'y pique* (Who opposes it gets hurt). Formed at Skipton-on-Swale, Yorks, September 25, 1943. Received Halifax B.IIIs from Nov '43 before re-equipping with Lancasters Jan '45.

434 (Bluenose) Squadron RCAF

Motto: *In excelsis vincimus* (We conquer in the heights). Formed at Tholthorpe, Yorks, June 13, 1943. Received Halifax B.Vs from June '43, moving to Croft, Co Durham, in Dec '43. B.IIIs arrived from May '44, but re-equipped with Lancasters Dec '44.

460 Squadron RAAF

Motto: *Strike and return.* Formed at Molesworth, Hunts, November 15, 1941. Received Halifax B.IIs between Aug and Oct '42 but not used on ops, replaced with Lancasters.

462 Squadron RAAF

No motto. Formed at Fayid, Suez Canal Zone in Egypt September 7, 1942, by amalgamation of No 10/227 and 76/462 Squadrons. Aug '43 squadron reformed at Driffield, Yorks, with Halifax B.IIIs within No 4 Group. B.IIIs from Aug '44 until Sept '45. Moved to Foulsham Dec '44 as part of 100 Group with 11 aircraft equipped with Airborne Cigar (ABC) and Carpet W/T jammer.

466 Squadron RAAF

No motto. Formed at Driffield, Yorks, October 15, 1942. Received Halifax B.IIs for training at Leconfield, Yorks, between Sept and Nov '43; B.IIIs back at Driffield between Oct '43 and May '45.

578 Squadron

Motto: *Accuracy.* Formed at Snaith, Yorks, January 14, 1944, equipped with Halifax B.IIIs. Moved to Burn, Yorks Feb '44 and disbanded Apr '45. VC awarded posthumously to Plt Off Cyril Barton following Nuremberg raid March '44 (see page 82). Two aircraft achieved over 100 missions, LW587 (104) and MZ527 (105).

614 (County of Glamorgan) Squadron

Motto: *Codaf I geislo* (I rise to search). Formed at Cardiff June 1, 1937, as Auxiliary Air Force unit. Received Halifax B.IIs Mar '44 when 462 (RAAF) Sqn was re-numbered 614 and based at Celone, Italy. Flew in target marking role. Replaced by Liberators in early '45.

640 Squadron

Formed at Leconfield, York, January 7, 1944, from C Flight 158 Sqn. Equipped with Halifax B.IIIs, initially from Lissett before returning to Leconfield. Between January '44 and disbandment in May '45, dropped 8,482 tons of bombs and won 4 Group Bombing Cup five times – more than any other squadron in Group.

Royal Air Force Coastal Command

58 Squadron

Motto: *Alis nocturnes* (On the wings of the night). Formed at Cramlington January 10, 1916. Received Halifax IIs for long-range maritime patrol Jan '43 based at Holmesley South and St Eval, Cornwall. Halifax IIIs from Apr to May '45.

202 Squadron

Motto: *Semper vigilate* (Be always vigilant). Formed at Eastchurch October 17, 1914. Received Halifax Met VIs at Aldergrove, NI, Oct '46 for meteorological duties. Replaced by Hastings May '51.

224 Squadron

Motto: *Fedel all'amico* (Faithful to a friend). Formed April 1, 1918. Received Halifax GR.VIs May '48 based at Aldergrove, NI; type withdrawn Mar '52, replaced by Shackletons.

502 Ulster Auxiliary Squadron

Motto: *Nihil timeo* (I fear nothing). Formed at Aldergrove May 15, 1925. Received Halifax II Srs IAs at St Eval, Cornwall, Jan '43 and IIIAs Dec '44. Disbanded Stornoway May '45.

Royal Air Force Transport Command

10 Squadron

Motto: *Rem acu tangere* (To hit the mark). Formed at Farnborough January 1, 1915. A bomber squadron during World War Two, No 10 transferred to TC May 7, '45, equipped with Dakotas in India. It acquired Halifax A.7s for heavy-lift duties before disbanding in Dec '47.

47 Squadron

Motto: *Nili nomen roboris omen* (The name of the Nile is the omen of our strength). Formed at Beverley March 1, 1916. After the war, squadron re-formed from 644 Sqn in Sept '46 at Qastina, Palestine, with Halifax A.9s and returned to Fairford, Glos. Operated in airborne and glider-towing role. Re-equipped with the first Hastings, Oct '48.

190 Squadron

Motto: *Ex tenebris* (Through darkness). Formed at Rochfield October 24, 1917. Became part of 38 Group Transport Command from Jan '44; received Halifax B.IIIs and VIIs May '45 before disbanding at Great Dunmow, Essex, Dec '45.

246 Squadron

Formed at Seaton Carew August 1918. Received Halifax IIIs Dec '44 to develop type on transport schedules – withdrawn Apr '45.

A 427 Sqn loss, Halifax B.V DK183 was shot down by a night-fighter near Texel following a raid on Bochum on June 12/13, 1943. Of the crew, four died and three became PoWs. (via Barry Charles Wheeler)

620 Squadron

Motto: *Dona ferentes adsumus* (We are coming bearing gifts). Formed at Chedburgh June 17, 1943. Received Halifax IIIs and VIIs at Great Dunmow, Essex, May '45. To Egypt and renumbered 113 Sqn in '46.

Special Duties

138 Squadron

Motto: *For freedom.* Formed at Newmarket August 25, 1941, for operations with Special Operations Executive (SOE). Halifax B.IIs from Dec '41. Halifax B.II Series 1A from Feb '43, some Vs in '44, based at Tempsford. Squadron to 3 Group Bomber Command end of '44.

148 Squadron

Motto: *Trusty.* Formed at Andover February 14, 1918. Special Liberator Flight at Gambut renumbered Mar '43 for Special Duties role with Liberator IIs and Halifax II Series Is and IAs operating from North African bases. Halifax Vs received Jul '44.

161 Squadron

Motto: *Liberate.* Formed at Newmarket February 14, 1942. Received Halifax II Series IAs and Vs from Dec '42 for agent dropping in North Africa. Replaced by Stirlings Sep '44.

295 Squadron

Motto: *In caelo auxilium* (Help from the skies). Formed at Netheravon August 1942 where Halifax Vs received Feb '43. Albemarles from Oct '43. In Feb '46 Halifax A.VIIs arrived at Tarrant Rushton with Mk IXs from Fairford Sep '47 and Oct '48.

296 Squadron

Motto: *Prepared for all things.* Formed from Glider Exercise Unit at Ringway January 25, 1942. Received Halifax Vs at Earl's Colne from October '44 followed by Mk IIIs from Feb '45. Operated on SOE drops, transport and bomber missions until disbanded January 23, 1946.

297 Squadron

Formed January 22, 1942, from Parachute Exercise Squadron Netheravon. Received Halifax Vs at Earl's Colne from Sept '44, followed by Mk IIIs from Feb '45 and A.7s and A.9s from Dec '45. Hastings from Oct '48.

298 Squadron

Motto: *Silent we strike.* Formed at Thruxton August 24, 1942. Received Halifax Vs at Tarrant Rushton for SOE ops Nov '43. Halifax IIIs in Oct '44 and VIIs in May '45. Disbanded in India Dec '46.

301 Squadron

Formed at Bramcote July 22, 1940. Halifax IIs Nov '44 for supply dropping to Polish Home Army. After Warwicks, Halifax C.8s took over Jan '46, disbanding in December.

304 Squadron

Formed as third Polish squadron in Bomber Command at Bramcote August 22, 1940. Halifax C.8s arrived May '46 and squadron disbanded Chedburgh in December.

624 Squadron

Formed at Blida September 22, 1943, with Halifax II Srs Is and Vs for agent dropping. Squadron changed role Dec '44.

644 Squadron

Motto: *Dentes draconis serimus* (We sow the dragon's teeth). Formed at Tarrant Rushton February 23, 1944, with Halifax Vs for SOE ops. Halifax IIIAs from Aug '44, Mk VIIs from Mar '45 and A.9s in Aug '46; disbanded Sept '46.

Meteorological Squadrons

517 Squadron

Formed at St Eval from No 1404 Met Flt August 11, 1943. Halifax Vs at St David's Nov '43 with Mk IIIs from Feb '45. Disbanded June '46.

518 Squadron

Formed at Stornoway July 9, 1943, with Halifax Vs. Mk IIIAs in Mar '45, with some VIs up to disbandment Oct '46.

519 Squadron

Formed from 1406 Met Flt at Wick August 15, 1943. Halifax IIIAs in Aug '45, remaining until disbandment at Leuchars May '46.

520 Squadron

Formed in Gibraltar September 20, 1943. Halifax Vs from Feb '44 and Mk IIIAs in Apr '45 until disbandment Apr '46.

521 Squadron

Formed at Bircham Newton, Norfolk, August 1, 1942. Halifax VIs in Dec '45 before disbandment at Chivenor Apr '46.

Miscellaneous units with Halifax aircraft

Bomber Command Instructors' School: Formed at Finningly December 5, 1944. Equipped with 11 Halifax B.IIIs and Vs, among other types.

Bombing Development Unit: Formed at Gransden Lodge July 20, 1942, with Halifax aircraft in addition to other types. Later to Feltwell (Feb '45) before Lindholme (Oct '45) and disbandment (Nov '45).

Bombing Trials Unit: Formed at West Freugh August 1, 1942. Halifax B.III received July '44.

Halifax Tow Conversion Unit: Formed at Holmsley South, Hants, November 15, 1944, within No 246 Sqn with Halifax IIIs. Disbanded at Merryfield March '45.

Airborne Forces Experimental Establishment: Formed February 15, 1942, at Ringway and disbanded September 1950. Flew a number of different aircraft including main marks of Halifax.

Air-Sea Warfare Development Unit: Former Coastal Command Development Unit, changed title January 1, 1945. Based Thorney Island in No 16 Group. Halifax II and III operated among a number of types. Disbanded April '70.

Bomber Command Instructors' School: Formed at Finningley December 5, 1944. Equipped with 11 Halifax III/Vs.

Bombing Development Unit: Formed at Gransden Lodge July 20, 1942. Established with 11 aircraft incl two Halifax, later three Halifax IIIs and one Mk VI from March '45. Disbanded Nov '45.

Central Gunnery School: Formed at Warmwell November 6, 1939. Halifax III used among many types.

Central Navigation School: Formed at Cranage August 14, 1942. Halifax B.III used among many types.

Coastal Command Development Unit: Formed at Carew Cheriton November 22, 1940. Halifax II among many types. (See Air-Sea Warfare Dev Unit.)

Conversion Flights: Affiliated to operational squadrons, each had establishment of four B.I/IIs. No 10 at Leeming formed Feb 17, 1942; No 35 at Linton-on-Ouse formed Jan 20, 1942; No 76 at Middleton St George formed Jan 20, 1942; No 102 at Dalton formed Jan 6, 1942; No 103 at Elsham Wolds formed May 2, 1942; No 158 at Linton-on-Ouse formed May 6, 1942; No 405 at Pocklington formed May 2, 1942; No 408 at Leeming formed Sept 20, 1942 (8 a/c); No 460 at Breighton formed May 22, 1942.

(Transport) Conversion Units: No 1331/1333 at Syerston, Dec '46–Jan '48, Halifax A.7s; No 1383 at Crosby-on-Eden, Aug '45–Aug '46, Halifax A.7s; No 1385 (Heavy Transport Support) at Wethersfield, Apr '46-Jul '46.

Heavy Conversion Units: Most had establishment between 16 and 36 Halifaxes. No 1652 at Marston Moor; No 1654 at Swinderby/Wigsley; No 1656 at Lindholme; No 1658 at Riccall; No 1659 at Leeming; No 1660 at Swinderby; No 1662 at Blyton; No 1663 at Rufforth; No 1664 at Croft; No 1665 at Mepal; No 1666 at Dalton; No 1667 at Lindholme; No 1668 at Balderton; No 1669 at Langar; No 1674 at Aldergrove.

Empire Air Navigation School: Formed at Shawbury October 1944. Establishment included 20 Halifax IIs.

Empire Flying School: Formed at Hullavington in May 1946. Halifax B.V.

Empire Radio School: Formed at Debden March 1946. Halifax B.6.

Flights: No 1341 (India); No 1361 (Meteorological); No 1363 (Met); No 1364 (Met); No 1418; No 1427; No 1445; No 1473; No 1474; No 1475; No 1485; No 1575 (Special Duties); No 1577; No 1586 (Special Duties); No 1589 Heavy Freight.

General Reconnaissance Aircraft Preparation Pool: Formed at Havorfordwest May 1944. Halifax GR.IIs for No 10 Gp. Disbanded Jan '46.

Halifax Development Flight: Formed at Holmsley South November 1944 within 246 Sqn. Disbanded Mar '45.

Heavy Glider Conversion Unit: No 21 formed at Brize Norton October 1944. Tug training with Halifax A.III/VII. Disbanded Dec '47.

Maintenance Units: No 13 at Henlow Camp (Halifax III/VI); No 20 at Aston Down (Halifax A.III); No 33 at Lyneham (Halifax V).

Meteorological Conversion Unit: Formed at Tiree in October 1943 to train Halifax Met crews. Disbanded Feb '44.

Middle East Training School: No 2, formed at Kabrit in May 1942. Disbanded Jun '43.

Operational Conversion Unit: No 241 formed at Dishforth in January 1948 to train crews for long-range transport squadrons. Halifax A.IX. Disbanded Apr '51.

Operational Training Unit (Coastal): No 1 formed at Siloth in April 1940. Halifaxes arrived July '43, but disbanded Oct; No 111 formed in Bahamas August 1942 (Halifax III/VIs).

Parachute Training School: Formed at Ringway February 1942. Used Halifax A.IXs.

Pathfinder Navigation Training Unit: Formed at Gransden Lodge April 1943 to train 8 Group crews. Disbanded Jun '45.

Radar Training Flight: Formed at Newmarket December 1943. Six Halifax II/V and two Lancasters.

Radio Warfare Establishment: Formed at Swanton Morley July 1945. Halifax IIIs withdrawn Apr '46.

Refresher Flying Unit: Formed at Haverfordwest May 1944. Halifax received Jun '44; disbanded Oct '44.

Transport Command Development Unit: Formed at Netheravon August 1945. Halifax A.III/IX & C.VIII. Disbanded Feb '57.

Squadron Codes

During the World War Two, RAF and Allied squadrons were generally allocated two or three-letter codes to identify their aircraft to other friendly units. From single-seat fighters to large bombers and transports, the codes provided a quick identifier as to which squadron the aircraft belonged and with an additional letter applied to the other side of the national marking, it also showed the individual aircraft within that squadron.

Halifax squadrons in Bomber, Coastal and other users, received the two-letter codes from a master listing at the Air Ministry and newly delivered aircraft were given the respective letters on both sides of the fuselage, usually to the left of the roundel with the individual aircraft letter on the right. As the war progressed and the number of flying units increased, so the two-letter codes began to give way to letter-number identifiers. The following listing doesn't pretend to be exhaustive but provides a quick reference to more than 100 operators of the Halifax from 1941 to 1950.

AL - 429 Sqn	JA - 1652 HCU	SE - 431 Sqn
BL - 1656 HCU	JF - 1654 HCU	SV - 1663 HCU
BM - 433 Sqn	J9 - 1668 HCU	TL - 35 Sqn
BY - 58 Sqn	KB - 1661 HCU	TT - 1668 HCU
C6 - 51 Sqn	KF - 1662 HCU	TV - 1660 HCU
C8 - 640 Sqn	KN - 77 Sqn	UG - 1654 HCU
DH - 1664 HCU	KR - 1667 HCU	VR - 419 Sqn
DT - 192 Sqn	KW - 425 Sqn	VU - 246 Sqn
DY - 102 Sqn	LK - 578/51 Sqn	V9 - 502 Sqn
D4 - 620 Sqn	LQ - 405 Sqn	XB - 224 Sqn
EK - 1656 HCU	L5 - 297 Sqn	X3 - 111 Cstal OTU
EQ - 408 Sqn	L6 - 1669 HCU	YW - 1660 HCU
EX - 199 Sqn	L8 - 347 Sqn	Y3 - 202/518 Sqn
EY - 78 Sqn	L9 - 190 Sqn	ZA - 10 Sqn
FCT - Emp Flg Scl	MA - 161 Sqn	ZB - 1658 HCU
FCX - Emp Flg Scl	MH - 51 Sqn	ZL - 427 Sqn
FD - 1659 HCU	MP - 76 Sqn	ZU - 1664 HCU
FEO - 21 HGCU	NA - 428 Sqn	Z5 - 462 Sqn
FET - 21 HGCU	NF - 138 Sqn	Z9 - 519 Sqn
FGC - Emp Nav Scl	ND - 1666 HCU	2K - 1668 HCU
FGE - Emp Nav Scl	NP - 158 Sqn/10 Con Flt	2P - 644 Sqn
FGF - Cent Nav Scl	NY - 1665 HCU	3G - 111 Cstal OTU
FGG - Cent Nav Scl	OG - 1665/1385 HCU	3J - 13 MU
FS - 148 Sqn	OO - 1663 HCU	5O - 521 Sqn
GG - 1667 HCU	OW - 426 Sqn	6F - 1669 HCU
GP - 1661 HCU	PE - 1662 HCU	6U - 415 Sqn
GR - 301 Sqn/SDF	PM - 103 Sqn	6Y - 171 Sqn
GY - 1383 Con Flt	PT - 420 Sqn	7C - 296 Sqn
G5 - 190 Sqn	P9 - ASWDU	8A - 298 Sqn
GV - 1652 HCU	QB - 424 Sqn	8E - 295 Sqn
HD - 466 Sqn	QD - 304 Sqn	8T - 298 Sqn
H3 - 111 Cstal OTU	QO - 432 Sqn	9U - 644 Sqn
H7 - 346 Sqn	QS - 620 Sqn	9W - 296 Sqn
IK - BC Inst Scl	QY - 1666 HCU	9X - 20 MU
IP - 434 Sqn	RV - 1659 HCU	

Abbreviations: ASWDU – Anti-Submarine Warfare Development Unit; BC Inst Scl – Bomber Command Instructors School; Cstal OTU – Coastal Command Operational Training Unit; Cent Nav Scl – Central Navigation School; Con Flt – Conversion Flight; Emp Flg Scl – Empire Flying School; Emp Nav Scl – Empire Navigation School; HCU – Heavy Conversion Unit; HGCU – Heavy Glider Conversion Unit; MU – Maintenance Unit; SDF – Special Duties Flight.

Chapter 17

Halifax Survivors

After the war and the last complete Halifaxes and Haltons had been broken up, little remained of the 6,178 aircraft which had contributed so much to the Allied victory, or the few converted airliner variants that helped restart UK post-war civil aviation.

The Halifax even eluded the clutches of the wartime Luftwaffe, as did the Lancaster, only wrecks of shot down examples providing the enemy with parts and sections instead of complete aircraft. Of the three heavy bombers in RAF service, only the Short Stirling was recovered and flown by the Germans, N3705 of 7 Sqn belly-landing near Gorinchem in the Netherlands after a mining sortie on August 16, 1942.

In Britain, its ancestral home, the only recognisable Halifax to survive was an engineless hulk with a single fin and rudder sitting on Radlett airfield in the late-1950s. Used by Standard Telephones & Cables for radio aerial trials, it was former Mk VII PN323 which had only accrued some ten hours flying before being delivered to No 29 MU at High Ercall for storage. After transferring to Radlett its crude appearance proved a source of passing interest for those travelling by train on the North-South railway line running alongside the airfield. By the end of 1961, it had gone, dismantled and scrapped like all the rest., the only surviving part being the nose section which was saved for eventual preservation by the Imperial War Museum in London.

Back from the Past

With the passing years, the absence of a complete Halifax in the national collection was a frustration for all those who served on the type. Then, early in 1970, word reached the RAF Museum that a virtually complete Halifax B.II was sitting on the floor of a lake in Norway. It turned out to be a 35 Sqn aircraft, W1048 which had been shot down on its first mission, an attack on the *Tirpitz* battleship on April 27, 1942.

Flown by a six-man crew led by Plt Off Donald McIntyre, 'S-Sugar' was hit by flak in the target area which started a fire in the starboard wing. Fearing the wing would break off, McIntyre skilfully put the burning aircraft down on a frozen lake near Hocklingen. Scrambling out of the fuselage, all but Sgt Vic Stevens, the flight engineer, who had injured his ankle and was forced to await the Germans, made their escape and evaded capture to return to England.

The fire in the starboard wing melted the ice and some 12 hours later the Halifax settled on the bottom of the lake. Thirty-one years later, in June

1973 a recovery team comprising members of the Norwegian Aviation Historical Society and the RAF Sub-Aqua Club led by Sgt David Walker from West Drayton cleared the silt from the wreck and fixed buoyancy bags and oil drums half-filled with air to the airframe and wings. Slowly, the lake gave up its prize and from 90ft down the almost complete aircraft, minus its outer starboard wing, finally emerged once again into daylight on the afternoon of June 30. As it broached the surface, the code-letters TL-S and the serial number were clearly visible.

Much work followed, including retrieval of the outer wing and engine, as the ravages of underwater exposure were halted. More than 8,000 rounds of live machine-gun ammunition were found inside the fuselage, while 31 years in the lake took its toll with the fabric control surfaces which had rotted away. A team from No 71 MU led by WO Jack Davis dismantled the remains and transported them back to England, courtesy of a British Army landing craft. Today, it rests much as it did on the lakebed floor in a place of honour at the RAF Museum Hendon. The decision was taken early on not to rebuild the combat veteran, but to leave it as a memorial to the brave men of Bomber Command.

A Yorkshire Restoration

A second Halifax was restored – or more correctly re-created – in the UK and today stands as a permanent reminder of the major Canadian and French involvement with the type. It forms part of the much-admired Yorkshire Air Museum (YAM) at Elvington, near York, an appropriate venue as this former base was home to two Free French squadrons in 1944 and 1945 (see Foreign-operated Halifaxes).

The basis of the exhibit is HR792, a Halifax GR.II of 58 Sqn which made a belly landing at Stornoway on January 13, 1945. Written off and broken up, the only surviving piece was the rear fuselage section which became a hen coop owned by Isle of Lewis resident, Robert McKenzie. When approached, he donated the rare surviving section to YAM and it was transported to Elvington for work to begin on the restoration in 1985, under the leadership of Ian Robertson.

New parts were manufactured by engineering trainees at British Aerospace Brough, and others were found following appeals – such as the framework from an original rear turret. The Armée de l'Air contributed a set of Bristol Hercules engines previously used by Nord Noratlas transports (although a Halifax GR.II powered by Merlins, the airframe had been built as a Hercules-powered B.III). The wings came from Handley Page Hastings C.1 TG536 located at Catterick, Frys Metals of Leeds manufactured

Above and right: From the mud and slime on the floor of Lake Hoklingen in Norway, the remarkably intact remains of the world's only Halifax lost on wartime operations came ashore in July 1973, 31 years from its force-landing after being hit by flak during an attack on the Tirpitz battleship. An early Mk II, W1048 now rests in the RAF Museum Hendon, displayed much as it was found as a memorial to the other aircraft and crews who did not return. (via Aeroplane)

new propeller blades, while the main wheels and tail wheel were recovered reasonably intact from a crash site near Paris in 1988.

Unveiled with much excitement at Elvington on September 13, 1996, the completed static exhibit looked almost indistinguishable from a wartime original. On the port side of its matt black fuselage were the markings of LV907 of 158 Sqn, the famous *Friday 13th*, and on the other side were the colours of No 347 Guyenne Free French Sqn.

Top, middle and left: These three pictures show the transformation of the Yorkshire Air Museum's Halifax B.III at Elvington from a garden shed to a completed aircraft. It stands as a memorial to the two Free French Halifax squadrons based at the airfield in 1944-45. A remarkable 'rebuild' by YAM members and helped by many people, the replica carries the colours of Friday the 13th on the port side and H7-N of 346 Free French squadron on the starboard. (via Aeroplane)

Canada remembers

The third Halifax survivor is at Trenton, Ontario. Like the Hendon aircraft, but not as complete, B.VII NA337 had force-landed following flak damage in a Norwegian lake, this time Lake Mjøsa, near the village of Stange, north of Oslo. The aircraft from 644 Sqn had been on a night mission to drop supplies to Norwegian Underground forces near Grue on April 23/24, 1945. Piloted by Flt Lt A Turnbull, NA337 successfully completed the airdrop and turning for home it was suddenly hit by accurate AA fire which shot out two of the engines forcing Turnbull to ditch the aircraft in Lake Mjøsa. The six crew survived the crash, but freezing temperatures took their toll and by morning only the rear gunner, Flt Sgt Thomas Weightman, had survived the night to be rescued and taken by the Germans as a PoW.

Fifty years later, a combined Canadian-Norwegian salvage team initiated work on bringing as many parts as possible up from the lake floor to produce a suitable memorial to the many Canadian aircrew lost on wartime operations. While the fuselage had been twisted on impact all those years before, the diving team managed to retrieve the tail unit and the engines, beginning on September 5, 1995. There to see the parts re-emerge was Thomas Weightman, the rear gunner.

The parts were taken back to the RCAF Memorial Museum at Trenton, Ontario, to start a ten-year restoration project. To assist with reconstructing the fuselage, the team travelled to Scotland and recovered a second rear fuselage from the Isle of Lewis, close to the location of the Yorkshire Air Museum's section, HR792. Other parts were specially made for the project, including the heavyweight Messier undercarriage legs.

A hall was built to accommodate the Halifax and the partially completed airframe was moved there in October 2004. Finally, on November 5, 2005, NA337 carrying 644 Sqn codes 2P-X was unveiled at Trenton in the presence of over 1,500 former Bomber Command veterans, many from No 6 (RCAF) Group.

Parts from two other Halifax crashes have been unearthed in recent years. In southern Poland, the remains of JP276 of 148 Special Duties Squadron were found in November 2006. A B.II, it was lost on August 4/5, 1944, during supply dropping operations in support of the Warsaw uprising.

Canadian interest has been shown in an attempt to raise the wreckage of a Met Flight Halifax which ditched in August 1945 off the Hebridean coast, west of Scotland. Returning from a weather patrol, B.III LW170 of 158 Sqn experienced a fuel leak and was forced to put down before regaining base. If it can be recovered, it will go to the Bomber Command Museum of Canada in Alberta.

Given the nation's significant involvement in Bomber Command operations, Canada has the third complete Halifax, a B.VII NA337 at the RCAF Museum at Trenton, Ontario. It too was recovered from Norway, Lake Mjosa giving up its treasure in September 1995. Ten years later, in November 2005, the rebuilt aircraft was unveiled at its permanent home. (Gordon McNulty)

Chapter 18

Handley Page Halifax Specifications

Type: Heavy bomber, crew 6-7. Mid-wing cantilever monoplane of all-metal stressed-skin construction. Wing built up of five main sections; centre-section carrying the inboard engine-mounting at its extremities, two intermediate sections, and two outer sections which carry the outboard engine mountings at their roots. The leading-edge of the outer sections is armoured and has balloon cable cutters. Ailerons have aluminium-alloy frames and fabric covering. Handley Page slotted trailing-edge flaps.

Fuselage is of oval shape in four main sections; max width, 5ft 6in; max depth, 9ft 6in.

Retractable undercarriage by Messier or Dowty on Mk V version. Wheels retract backwards into inner engine-nacelles leaving small portion of each wheel protruding when doors closed. Track, 24ft 8in. Retractable tailwheel on later versions.

Tail unit with two spars, twin fins and rudders. Trim tabs in all control surfaces.

Tailplane span, 30ft 4in.

Halifax Costs

The prototype HP.57 Halifax cost Handley Page between £85,000-£90,000 to design and build. Production models were costed at around £12,500 each.

HP.57 Halifax B.I	
Powerplant	Four 1,130hp Rolls-Royce Merlin X engines. Fuel capacity, 1,392 gal (6,328 lit).
Dimensions	Span 98ft 10in (30.21m); length, 70ft 1in (21.36m); height, 20ft 9in (6.37m); wing area, 1,200sq ft (111.4sq m).
Performance	Max speed, 265mph (426km/h) at 17,500ft (5,334m); initial climb rate, 750ft/min (3.81m/sec); service ceiling, 18,000ft (5,490m); range with bomb-bay fuel and 5,800lb (2,633kg) bomb load, 1,860 miles (2,993km). Weight, empty, 33,860lb (15,372kg); gross, 55,000lb (24, 970kg).
Armament	Two 0.303in guns in Boulton-Paul Type C nose turret, four 0.303in guns in B-P Type E tail turret fed by ammunition tracks from magazines aft of mid-upper turret, two Vickers K-guns in beam hatches on B.I Series 2. Max bomb load, 13,000lb (5,900kg) carried in main 22ft (6.7m) long fuselage compartment and three inner wing cells each side.

HP.59 Halifax B.II	
Powerplant	Four 1,139hp R-R Merlin XX engines. Fuel capacity, 1,882 gal (8,556 lit).
Dimensions	As for B.I.

HP.59 Halifax B.II	
Performance	As for B.I except max weight, 60,000lb (27,200kg).
Armament	As for B.I except beam guns replaced with two 0.303in guns in B-P Type C turret in mid-upper position.

HP.59 Halifax B.II Series I (Special)

As for B.II except interim nose fairing replacing nose turret. Mid-upper turret deleted

HP.59 Halifax B.II Series IA	
Powerplant	Four 1,390hp R-R Merlin 22 engines with four-bladed propellers. Low drag nacelles with Morris radiators.
Dimensions	As for B.I except length extended to 71ft 7in (21.85m).
Performance	As for B.II except gross weight to 65,000lb (29,510kg).
Armament	As for B.II except transparent nose fairing replacing turret with mounting for one hand-held 0.303in Vickers K-gun. Four 0.303in guns in B-P Type A mid-upper turret. Bomb-bay doors fitted with more efficient seals and typical load included provision for two 4,000lb (1,818kg) bombs or a single 8,000lb (3,636kg) weapon. Late-production aircraft delivered with D-type fins and rudders to cure 'rudder stall' problem.

HP.59 Halifax GR.II Series I & IA	
Powerplant	As for B.II Series IA. Fitted with three and/or four-blade propellers.
Dimensions	As for B.II Series IA.
Performance	Max speed, 250mph (402km/h) at 13,000ft (3,965m); service ceiling, 21,000ft (6,405m); range, 1,660 miles (2,671km). Weight, empty 35,577lb (16,152kg); loaded, 60,000lb (27,200kg).
Armament	Single Browning 0.50in gun in nose, four 0.303in guns in tail turret, B-P Type A mid-upper turret with four 0.303in guns, and optional Frazer-Nash FN.64 turret or Preston-Green 0.50in gun in ventral mount.

HP.61 Halifax B.III	
Powerplant	Four 1,615hp Bristol Hercules XVI radial engines. Fuel capacity, 1,986 gal (9,028 lit).
Dimensions	Span, 104ft 2in (31.75m); length, 71ft 7in (21.85m); height, 21ft 7in (6.6m). Wing area, 1,200sq ft (111.5sq m).
Performance	Max speed, 282mph (454km/h); cruise speed, 241mph (149km/h); ceiling, 24,000ft (7,770m); range, 2,350 miles (3,780km); climb to 20,000ft (6,097m) in 42min. Weight, loaded, 64,000lb (29,056kg).
Armament	As GR.II Series I/IA, plus single 0.50in gun in Preston-Green ventral mount. Max bomb load, 10,000lb (4,540kg) in fuselage and 3,000lb (1,362kg) in wing cells. H2S radar in ventral position.

HP.60A Halifax B.IV

Projected development of Mk II with 1,280hp R-R Merlin 60s with long-tailed inner nacelles and enlarged tail unit. Prototype only (HR756).

HP.63 Halifax B.V

As B.II but Dowty main undercarriage replacing Messier units. Production totalled 658 by Rootes Securities and 246 by Fairey Aviation at Stockport. Used by No 6 Group (RCAF) squadrons. Conversions to GR.V and Met Mk V for Coastal Command. Others served with Airborne Forces as glider tugs.

HP.61 Halifax B.VI	
Powerplant	Four 1,675hp Bristol Hercules 100 radial engines. Fuel capacity, 2,190 gal (9,956 lit) plus optional three 690 gal (3,137 lit) tanks in bomb-bay.
Dimensions	Span (extended wing tips), 104ft 2in (31.75m); length 71ft 7in (21.85m); height, 21ft 7in (6.6m). Wing area, 1,275sq ft (118.3sq m).
Performance	Max speed, 312mph (502km/h) at 22,000ft (6,706m) and 290mph (497km/h) at 10,500ft (3,200m); cruising speed, 218-260mph (351-418km/h) at 20,000ft (6,100m); service ceiling at max weight, 24,000ft (7,315m); range, 1,260 miles (2,027km) with max bombs, 2,400 miles (3,867km) with max fuel. Weight, empty, 39,000lb (17,706kg); gross, 68,000lb (30, 872kg).
Armament	As for B.III.

HP.61 Halifax B.VII	
Powerplant	Four 1,615hp Bristol Hercules XVI radial engines.
Dimensions	As for B.VI.
Performance	Max speed, 320mph (515km/h) at 22,000ft (6,705m); cruising speed, 272mph (437km/h) at 20,000ft (6,096m); service ceiling, 24,000ft (8,179m); range, 1,660 miles (2,671km/h) with full fuel and 5,800lb (2,631kg) bomb load.
Armament	Single 0.303in Vickers K-gun in nose, B-P Type A mid-upper turret with four Browning 0.303in guns, B-P Type E tail turret with four Browning 0.303in guns. Max bomb load, 13,000lb – typical load, one 500lb bomb in each of six wing bays, two 2,000lb + six 1,000lb bombs in fuselage bay. H2S radar in ventral position.

HP.70 Halifax C.VIII	
Powerplant	Four 1,650hp Bristol Hercules 100 radial engines, each driving a DH three-blade constant-speed fully-feathering airscrew.
Dimensions	As B.VI except length 73ft 7in (22.45m).
Performance	Max speed, 320mph (512km/h); economical cruising speed at 10,000ft (3,050m), 200mph (320km/h); range at 65,000lb (29,510kg) all up weight, 1,810 miles (2,896km); range with normal fuel and load of 7,750lb (3,518kg), 2,539 miles (4,050km). Max range with extra tanks in place of pannier, 3,510 miles (5,616km). Tare weight, 37,750lb (17,140kg); basic equipped, 40,600lb (18,434kg).
Accommodation	Ten stretchers or 11 passengers or paratroops in rear cabin, plus 8,000lb (3,632kg) capacity detachable freight pannier in bomb-bay. Crew of five and dual controls.

HP.70 Halton	
Powerplant	Four 1,675hp Bristol Hercules 100 radial engines, each driving a DH Hydromatic three-blade fully-feathering airscrew. Max fuel capacity, 2,379gal (10,821lit); normal fuel capacity, 2,190gal (9,962lit).
Dimensions	Span 103ft 8in (31.60m); length 73ft 7in (22.44m); height, 20ft 8in (6.30m). Wing area, 1,275sq ft (118.4sq m).
Performance	Max speed, 320mph (512km/h); max cruise speed, 270mph (434km/h) at 15,000ft (4,570m); initial rate of climb, 740ft/min (226m/min); service ceiling, 21,000ft (6,400m); range with normal fuel tankage, 2,530 miles (4,071km). Max loaded weight, 65,000lb (29,482kg); max payload, 10,500lb (4,763kg).
Accommodation	In BOAC service, ten passengers in upholstered rear compartment, five each side. Ventral baggage pannier with 8,000lb (3,629kg) capacity.

HP.71 Halifax A.IX	
Powerplant	Four 1,675hp Bristol Hercules XVI radial engines. Fuel capacity, 2,772 gal (12,600 lit)
Dimensions	Span, 103ft 8in (31.60m); length, 71ft 7in (21.85m); height 21ft 7in (6.6m).
Performance	Max speed, 289mph (465km/h) at 13,500ft (4,117m); service ceiling, 20,000ft (6,096m). Tare weight, 39,750lb (18,068kg); max take-off, 65,000lb (29,482kg).
Armament	B-P Type D tail turret mounting twin 0.50in (12.7mm) machine-guns with gun-laying radar.

Other books you might like:

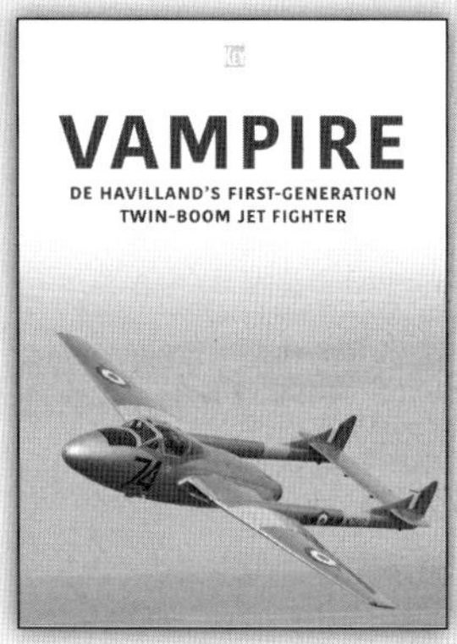

Historic Military Aircraft
Series, Vol. 26

Historic Military Aircraft
Series, Vol. 23

Historic Military Aircraft
Series, Vol. 22

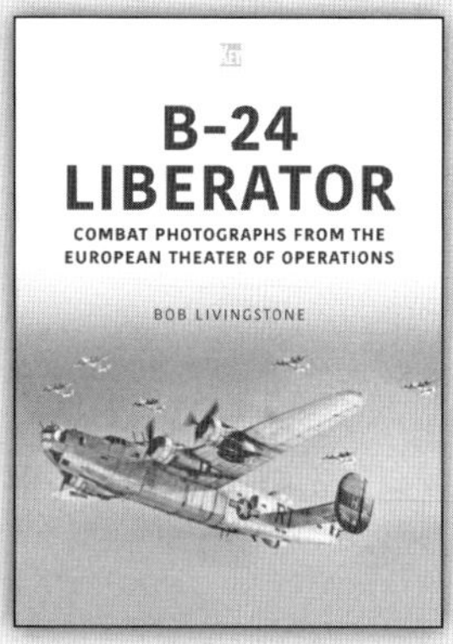

Historic Military Aircraft
Series, Vol. 21

Historic Military Aircraft
Series, Vol. 20

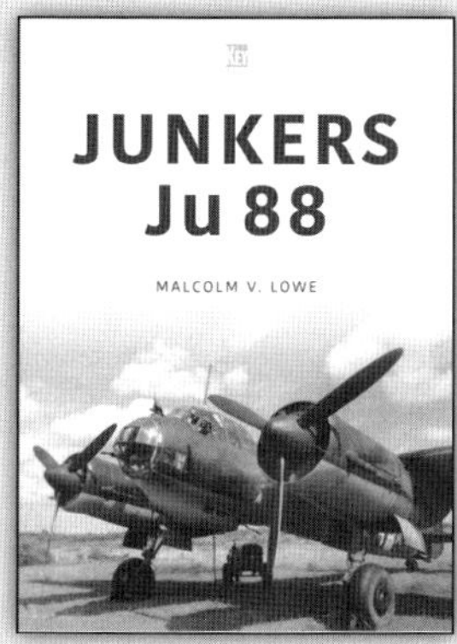

Historic Military Aircraft
Series, Vol. 15

For our full range of titles please visit:
shop.keypublishing.com/books

VIP Book Club
Sign up today and receive
TWO FREE E-BOOKS

Be the first to find out about our forthcoming
book releases and receive exclusive offers.

Register now at **keypublishing.com/vip-book-club**

*Our VIP Book Club is a 100% spam-free zone, and we will never share your email with anyone else.
You can read our full privacy policy at: privacy.keypublishing.com*